DOSSIER

DOSSIER

The Secret Files
They Keep on *You*

ARYEH NEIER

STEIN AND DAY/*Publishers*/New York

Portions of Chapter 8 appeared in slightly different form in the author's article, "Marked for Life: Have You Ever Been Arrested?" in the April 15th, 1973 issue of *The New York Times Magazine*.

Grateful acknowledgment is made for permission to use the following: Excerpt from "The Unknown Citizen" by W. H. Auden. Copyright 1940 and renewed 1968 by W. H. Auden from COLLECTED SHORTER POEMS 1927-1957, reprinted by permission of Random House, Inc.

Acknowledgments

Many of my colleagues in the ACLU, who are also engaged in the struggle against dossiers, were generous in sharing with me information they had gathered and in helping me in many other ways. Among them were David Addlestone, Frank Askin, Alvin Bronstein, Kate Cunningham, Dorothy Davidson, Hope Eastman, Arthur Eisenberg, Bruce Ennis, Matthew Feinberg, Leon Friedman, Ira Glasser, Jeremiah Gutman, Chris Hansen, Susan Hewman, Florence Isbell, Tom Kerr, Douglass Lea, Alan Levine, Charles Marson, Marion Miller, Stephen Nagler, Burt Neuborne, Joseph Remcho, Linda Ruderman, Herman Schwartz, Jeanette Sharples, Robert Smith, Ralph Temple, and Rena Uviller. I gratefully acknowledge their help. I owe special thanks to John Shattuck, who has served as counsel in many of the court cases discussed in this book. I drew very heavily on his insights, his knowledge, and his files. Frank Donner, a walking encyclopedia of information on political surveillance, was also particularly helpful, and I greatly enjoyed my long and rambling conversations with him.

The staff of the U.S. Senate Subcommittee on Constitutional Rights has done an excellent job of ferreting out information on dossier building. By exposing the activities of the executive branch of the federal government to the light of day, they have stopped some of its wilder excesses and paved the way for privacy legislation. I have been helped greatly by the work of the committee's chief counsel, Lawrence Baskir, and his associates on the committee staff. The retirement of the committee chairman, Senator Sam Ervin of North Carolina, deprives the Congress of its most effective voice for privacy. I hope others will try to fill his shoes.

To Jeannette Hopkins, who suggested I write this book, I am very grateful. Among other things, her editorial guidance has spared readers from many detours and digressions.

Finally, I am grateful for the forbearance of my wife Yvette and son David. This book was written in time grudgingly stolen from their company.

—ARYEH NEIER

Contents

He was found by the Bureau
    of Statistics to be
One against whom there was no
    official complaint,
And all the reports on his conduct agree
That, in the modern sense of an old-fashioned
    word, he was a saint . . .
Was he free? Was he happy? The
    question is absurd:
Had anything been wrong, we should certainly
    have heard.

"The Unknown Citizen"
W. H. Auden

Introduction

The Dossier-Mongers

Over the years, I have accumulated my share of derogatory records. I have been arrested. My Selective Service file contains a notice from the ROTC at Cornell that I am not suitable officer material because of my negative attitude toward military training. I once got into a dispute with a credit card company that almost ended in a lawsuit—litigation was staved off when the company conceded I was right. They then refunded a little more than I thought was due to me. A number of public and private organizations think the American Civil Liberties Union, of which I am executive director, is subversive and, no doubt, they keep an extensive dossier on me. There is probably a lot more I have forgotten or never knew about. For these reasons, I have very personal grounds for being angry about dossiers. For similar reasons, I think almost everybody else should be similarly angry.

One of the satisfactions I get from my work for the ACLU is the ability to do something about dossiers and dossier-mongers. It has consumed much of my time and energy for more than a decade. It has been especially satisfying recently because there is more organized effort now to curb dossiers than ever before. Not much has been accomplished yet, but I have a sense of impending success. This book was written in the hope that it would help quicken the movement. It will if it makes you angry. Here is a sample of the outrage I am angry about—it could happen—maybe it is already happening to you:

• A member of the faculty of an Ivy League college discovered that her auto insurance policy had been canceled. The Retail Credit Company had given her a bad report card—she had been living in the same house with a man "without the benefit of wedlock." What her private life had to do with careful driving was never explained. The dossier-mongers had been at work.

• At an Eastern college, the chief switchboard operator had a dangerous mission from the FBI—she was assigned as an undercover informer to monitor the long-distance phone calls of a professor of philosophy. Thousands of other such operatives are scavenging for scraps to insert in the dossiers of unwary Americans.

• In Yorba Linda, California, teachers are passing judgment on children by diagnosing who is a "predelinquent," and predicting who has the potential for future crime. The alarming symptom noted in one nine-year-old girl included short attention span, pilfering of pencils, and "an inability to have fun." The stigma carefully recorded in Juanita's dossier may follow her all her life. She could be your child or mine.

• In Maryland, thousands of boys, most of them black and poor, were subjected to blood tests to determine—on the basis of the flimsiest of scientific speculation—whether they had chromosomes that cause violent behavior. A lawsuit interrupted the testing, but it began again. Dossiers grow like weeds: it is hard to eradicate them once they take root.

• An eleven-year-old boy in Queens joined with friends in burning make-believe draft cards in imitation of an anti-Vietnam demonstration. A policeman issued a Y.D. (Youth Division) card for causing an unauthorized fire. As a result, Michael was forced out of the school honor guard and out of his job as fifth-grade reporter for the school newspaper. Obviously a dangerous criminal, Michael found his career halted just in time to protect society. The dossier-mongers never rest.

• A Vietnam veteran, whose eye was injured in a bomb explosion, was denied a request for medical attention—he has since lost his eye. He cannot even afford a glass eye. His combat medals made no difference to a callous and ungrateful government. While stationed at Fort Knox, Kentucky, he had disgraced the service by going home for Christmas one day early.

• A top school official lives in fear that her life and career will be destroyed by a dossier. In her youth, years ago, she had been briefly married to a man who had been arrested on a relatively minor charge. More than twenty years, a new marriage, a Ph.D., and a prominent career later, she is terrified today that someone will comb through their files and find her name.

Millions of Americans, all who read this book among them, are potential victims of the dossier-scavenger. Somewhere there is a file on you as there is on me.

These stories could be multiplied millions of times over. The all-seeing eye leaves no one out except, perhaps, pool hustlers!

But they pay for their privacy. When three winners in a Las Vegas hotel won prizes in a pool tournament, the management insisted on Social Security numbers before it would pay. The hustlers had no numbers to give. They had no dossiers. They also did not get paid! Hustling is a profession which generally requires no filling out of forms, no examination, no license or union membership. Hustlers don't pay taxes. They rarely have dependents. They avoid transactions such as the purchase of homes, which would compel them to furnish biographical information. They own no credit cards, or at least, none to which they are legally entitled.

When hustlers are driven by economic exigency to seek to moonlight in other trades, they are out of luck—no Social Security numbers, no pay. But most of us are not hustlers by trade, we are "lucky." We are on public record.

Numerous organizations devote much or all of their time to collecting dossiers on us. The FBI files about 200 million fingerprint cards, including many on persons long dead. The Medical Information Bureau, a private organization serving the insurance industry, has the medical and psychiatric records of 12½ million Americans.

In the summer of 1974, the United States Senate Subcommittee on Constitutional Rights reported that 54 federal agencies it had surveyed maintained 858 data banks on individual Americans; 765 of the data banks had 1,245,699,494 records. The committee got no figures on the number of records in the remaining 93 banks. The committee scrutinized the operations of all the dossier collectors except some of the very large number administered by the army. Eighty-four percent of the data banks were operating without explicit authority in law.

The Senate committee flatly labeled as "blacklists" the army's Worldwide Automated Military Police Operations and Information System; the Department of Housing and Urban Development's Debarred Bidders List; the Federal Communications Commission's Checklist; the Securities and Exchange Commission's Name and Relationship System; the State Department's Passport Lookout File; and the Department of Transportation's Deterrence of Air Piracy System and its National Driver Register. The Department of Justice keeps seven of the "blacklists." They are the Internal Security Division's file on "Civil Disobedience"; the Organized Crime Intelligence System; the FBI's National Crime Information Center Wanted Persons file; the FBI Known Professional Check Passer files; and three Law Enforcement Assistance Administration–funded files on Wanted Persons, Organized Crime, and Civil Disorders.

The Treasury Department has nine "blacklists": the Customs Bureau's TECS/CADPIN system; four Internal Revenue Service Intelligence files; the IRS Special Service Staff files; and the Secret Service files. Others include the Office of the Inspector General file in the Department of Agriculture; the air force's Unfavorable

Information files; the Federal Deposit Insurance Corporation's Section 8 and 19 files; the General Services Administration's Debarred Bidders Lists; and the Small Business Administration's Investigative Records of "character checks" on dubious applicants.

These are acknowledged dossiers, collected and nurtured about persons federal agencies have specifically marked for discrimination or surveillance. Mongers keep many other dossiers replete with derogatory information. The files on drug addicts maintained by several federal agencies and the FBI's Identification Division, the nation's central depository of arrest records, are among them. Add to these the unacknowledged files or those reputedly destroyed. Among these are the army's giant political surveillance files and the Department of Health, Education and Welfare's blacklist of politically suspect scientists who are supposed to be denied research grants.

The federal government has no monopoly on data gathering. State and local governments and private enterprise are building bigger and better dossiers. The Senate committee's survey itself was limited to the executive branch of the federal government and, therefore, left out Congressional dossiers like the extensive files accumulated over several decades by the House Internal Security Committee and its predecessor, the House Un-American Activities Committee.

A brisk traffic goes on among all of these various scavenging institutions. They exchange data on people they regard as troublemakers. Once a person is so labeled, many institutions will make trouble for him. He will be denied a job, a home, credit or insurance. He may be arrested solely because he has acquired the "troublemaker" label.

Since the Korean War, more than two million men have left the armed services with less than honorable discharges or with dishonorable code numbers on their honorable discharge papers. They pay for that all their lives. Schools exclude a million children because they are considered "behavior problems" or because they are labeled as mentally or physically handicapped. Arrest records identify some 35 million Americans, most of whom have never been convicted of any crime. Some young children are labeled as "predelinquents" because it is *anticipated* that they will become troublemakers.

The "troublemaker" label on the dossier turns many Americans into fugitives. They try to escape the scarlet letter by moving to a new place, hoping the records of their misdeeds, real and fancied, will not follow them. Sometimes, they succeed, but, often, the records catch up with them and they move on again.

New York, Chicago, and Detroit were once the top attractions for Americans on the run—big cities, with lots of jobs, where a person could get lost. Fugitive Americans now favor sun-belt cities like Miami, Albuquerque, Los Angeles, San Francisco, Denver, and Phoenix, like the "golden city" of Mahagonny in the opera by Bertolt Brecht and Kurt Weill, for the "discontented of all the continents." As the discontented move to American golden cities, those cities acquire the highest crime rates. The fastest growing city of them all, Albuquerque, has the highest rate in the country.

This book examines how public and private institutions— schools, hospitals, the armed services, law enforcement agencies, and credit bureaus—go about building dossiers that create troublemakers and harass us all. The book's thesis is that these dossiers invade privacy, limit opportunities to get ahead, and defeat us in our efforts to survive.

Dossier-building is at odds with the idea of a free society. It also brings about just what it tries to prevent—a nation of troublemakers. The dossiers THEY are keeping on you and me follow us everywhere. They violate our private lives, they damage and stigmatize our children. They keep us from jobs, from mortgages, from bank loans. They may put us behind bars even when we are innocent. Dossiers may tell lies about us, and those lies may haunt us all our lives.

1

"A Real Sickie ... Have Fun"
SCHOOL RECORDS

A real sickie—abs., truant, stubborn & very dull. Is verbal only about outside irrelevant facts. Can barely read (which was a large accomplishment to get this far). Have fun!

A New York City school teacher inserted that callous description in a child's school dossier to introduce him to his next teacher. The record was, of course, "confidential." "Confidential" has a meaning in this context opposite to what it usually conveys. In the parlance of most schools, a "confidential" record is not revealed to a child or his parents; it *is* accessible to virtually anyone else. A negative record, as many are, can make official harassment of children self-perpetuating. The child is condemned to failure before his life has a chance to begin.

A substitute teacher in Colorado came upon her own son's school record by chance. The boy, then in the sixth grade, "has Marxist tendencies" according to a notation entered by a fifth-grade teacher. The Colorado ACLU got the record expunged. Education writer Diane Divoky has been collecting other examples of school records meant to be kept secret from children and their parents. In one case, a community tutoring project's secretary called a school to find out what grade a child was in. The principal responded to the request and offered the additional information from the record that the child was a bed-wetter and his mother an alcoholic with many boyfriends. A mother of a junior high school boy sneaked a look at another school record. She found that a teacher in second grade had said her son had exhibitionist tendencies. After considerable effort the woman tracked down the teacher who had, by then, left the school system. The "exhibitionist tendencies" label had been pinned on her son because of a single incident in which he had rushed out of a lavatory unzipped.

Schools have been compiling dossiers since the early part of the nineteenth century, but only in the last half century have records begun to include information beyond grades and attendance. The psychological observations which taint today's school records reflect a reformist impulse to deal with the "whole child." In 1925, a National Education Association committee recommended that schools maintain a wide variety of records on students: teacher's daily register book, pupil's general cumulative record, pupil's health and physical records, guidance record, pupil's psychological record, and principal's office record.

In 1968, under the auspices of the Russell Sage Foundation, David A. Goslin and Nancy Bordier looked into school practices in compiling and disseminating records. They sent questionnaires to superintendents of sixty-eight school districts and received completed questionnaires from fifty-four districts in twenty-nine states. A majority of the school districts responding acknowledged they allowed prospective employers, juvenile courts (without subpoena), local police, the health department, the CIA, and the FBI access to the records. Only a small minority would allow access to such information to children or their parents.

If anything, the survey understated the accessibility of the files. Even when a school superintendent states as policy that the file is not available to a prospective employer or a policeman, an individual school principal may provide it. Furthermore, many schools which deny direct inspection of files are willing to describe what is in them ("This kid is a real troublemaker").

Publicity resulting from the publication of the Russell Sage study prompted the New York City school system in 1970 to create a special committee of school officials and representatives of civic organizations to review the problem of records and to recommend new policies. The committee called for a denial of school records to outsiders, and such an order was put into effect. Anguished protests immediately arose from the Council of Supervisory Associations, which represents the deans and principals in the New York City schools. The policy was rescinded fifteen days later. In that brief intervening period, twenty-eight separate categories of outside groups which had previously obtained access to the records complained about the elimination of their usual sources of information. They included the armed services, the FBI, police, welfare and probation officials, the Selective Service System, the Civil Service Commission, and district attorneys. Several court cases later, prohibitions on outside access were restored.

Parents of New York City school children are now able to see the "confidential" records on their children and contest their accuracy. A handful of states and local school districts elsewhere in the country have adopted similar rules. Perhaps the best rules were adopted by the State Board of Education in New Mexico in February 1972. They give the student "the right to inspect" his record and "an explanation of any information recorded on it." Faculty and administrative officers of the school must "demonstrate a need to know" before seeing a student's record. Government agencies may obtain date and place of birth, school and class in which the student is enrolled, dates of enrollment, and the name and address of parent or guardian. Nothing else can be obtained by a government agency without written authorization from the student or on the basis of a court order which the student has been notified about and can challenge. Other persons and organizations can get information beyond the fact and dates of enrollment only when the student consents in writing.

In most communities, parents learn what is in their children's school dossiers only under very unusual circumstances.

Mark Isaacs, a professor of communications at Temple University, saw his eight-year-old son David's school records only after David was killed in a highway accident. The records emerged during the litigation that followed. In David's file, Mark Isaacs found the following comment from a school psychologist:

Although David was generally cooperative, he became very argumentative and disrespectful when his date of birth was questioned. Although it was listed as 1-22-62 on the cumulative folder, he insisted it was changed to 7-4-61. David also gives the impression that he had a feeling of superiority and perfection. He stated that his mother said he read well at home. Up to this point the parent-school rapport hasn't been too good. Perhaps David's feelings of superiority, if they do exist, are bolstered through parent attitudes. . . .

In an article for the *Philadelphia Inquirer,* the grieving but outraged father described his reactions:

My wife and I have tried to recall situations in which we had proved unmanageable.

We have come up with three: (1) I refused to fill out a questionnaire from a commercial insurance company that had worked out a special accident policy deal with the school board; (2) I also refused to answer questions about my income in a survey designed to justify federal contributions to the district; and (3) my wife refused to go along with a teacher who wanted David punished on weekends by barring him from his two or three favorite TV programs—this was when he did not do his reading to the teacher's satisfaction. My wife's answer in the third case was that she saw no virtue in ganging up on the kid.

My answer in the first instance was that I had been evading insurance deals for years and in the second that my income was not any of the school's business. But David was in tears when I refused to fill out the forms. He said the teacher would be angry with him. I pooh-poohed that and told him to ask her or the principal to call me, if he were given a hard time.

As for the changed birth date, David was unhappy about being the youngest boy in the third grade. His father had a solution:

For some reason the convention of the Queen's birthday popped into my head. Queen Elizabeth's actual birthday is in April, but takes place in May or June, when the weather is better for a garden party. What was good enough for her Majesty was certainly good enough for my son.

The school psychologist could not be expected to know why David Isaacs said his birthday had been changed. If that information had to be in David's record at all, a dubious proposition, the mystery would have been solved if anyone had bothered to ask David's parents. Except for David Isaacs' death, the dossier would have remained a secret, that is, to Mr. and Mrs. Isaacs, but not to college admissions officers, personnel directors, and others who would form their impressions of David from these derogatory notes.

Dossiers of a number of children came to light through the court cases leading to adoption of the New York City rules allowing parents access to their children's records. One black girl in a sixth-grade class for intellectually gifted children was described by her records as, "Eager to succeed in class—works very hard at her school assignments," but by a different teacher, as, "Extremely hostile, anti-social behavior—Does not socialize with children of other races or background." Another record described a girl's father as, "Attractive, well dressed, verbal—black militant—very hostile." This is the kind of unfriendly and gratuitous —and probably false—information schools are now collecting for the benefit of future employers and others in a position to damage.

A student handbook published at Jamaica High School in New York City advised students on such matters as behavior in assemblies ("During the assembly program, if there is occasion for approval, applaud politely"), and warned them that employers "want to know whether you have been able to get along with your classmates and teachers. . . . Long after you have been graduated, inquiries concerning your record are answered by consulting your record card. *This is truly a permanent one.* Make it a good one." Applaud politely.

Jamaica High School inserted in David Shakin's "permanent" record a notation that he criticized the absence of civil liberties in the school on a radio program broadcast outside the school. With the help of the attorney who directed the New York Civil Liberties Union's Student Rights Project, Alan H. Levine, Shakin took the matter to court. He won an unprecedented decision wiping out the reference to the radio program from the record. The decision infuriated the school principal. He complained, in a memorandum to the faculty, that the court order would "grant complete immunity to any youngster to say anything he pleases, anywhere, at anytime."

The Shakin case was only one episode in what became a heated controversy over the subject of dossiers between the Civil Liberties Union and the several organizations which represent New York school principals. Two weeks before Sandra Wilson was due to graduate from Junior High School 62 in New York City, her mother received a letter from the school announcing that Sandra would be barred from the graduation exercises because of "a consistent lack of good citizenship during the past three years." Instead of getting a diploma, Sandra was to get a "Certificate of Attendance and Transfer." The school refused to allow Sandra's mother to inspect the anecdotal record on which the judgment of "bad citizenship" had been based.

Ms. Wilson challenged the denial of a diploma in a proceeding before the New York State Commissioner of Education. The New York City Elementary School Principals Association, entering the case, called on the commissioner to uphold the denial of a diploma. "Compulsory disclosure to parents of such teacher notes," the principals said, "would be contrary to the best interests of the children . . . it would make guidance counsellors and teachers reluctant to enter in their working notes observations, evaluations, and opinions which parents may seek to dispute, and to demand retraction or correction."

The commissioner was not persuaded that Sandra Wilson's best interests would be served if her mother was unable to find out why she was not to get a diploma. He dismissed the principals' argument, "There is no merit in this contention. . . . It is readily apparent that no one has a greater right to such information than the parent."

About the same time, Louis Carroll, a good student and president of the Student Organization, was denied his diploma by Evander Childs High School in the Bronx, also for "bad citizenship." The New York Civil Liberties Union won a ruling in the Carroll case, ending the power of school principals to condition graduation upon citizenship. "It is not the prerogative of the school system," the chancellor of the Board of Education ruled, "to manipulate the award of a diploma when the facts clearly indicate that the diploma—an award for academic achievement—has in fact been earned. In brief, the school is empowered to grant diplomas not citizenship."

That was too much for the High School Principals Association. "Students who have been robbed, mugged, assaulted or lured into drug use," said the principals, "will see a perpetrator receive his diploma along with them at graduation." A *New York Times* editorial labeled this "an emotional reaction which . . . only exacerbates misunderstanding over the issue of discipline." That prompted the president of the High School Principals Association to send a letter to the editor citing a horrible example. "Perhaps one case may be cited," he wrote, "in which a diploma was withheld this past June. In his last term the student cut classes at will, was deliberately insubordinate, used abusive language to school officials and walked out of activities that depended upon him. The counseling offered him was ignored."

Cutting classes, using abusive language, and ignoring counseling are not quite in the same class as the robberies, muggings, and assaults conjured up by the principals in the statement which drew the *Times*'s criticism of "emotional reaction." The sharply scaled-down list of sins is symptomatic of the whole problem with anecdotal records. They are unproven conclusory statements not ordinarily subject to inspection and challenge.

Growing nationwide interest in the school records problem was reflected in a May 14, 1974, vote in the U.S. Senate to withhold federal funds from any school which does not protect the privacy of school records. The action came in the form of an amendment to the federal aid to education bill offered by Senator James Buckley of New York. It was adopted by voice vote with virtually no opposition.

The Buckley amendment says parents may review "any and all official records, files and data directly related to their children" and "shall have an opportunity for a hearing to challenge the content of their child's school record." The amendment would deny federal funds to any school "which has a policy of permitting the release of records or files of students without the written consent of their parents." Unhappily, this section contains an exception for all officials of the school the child attends and officials of any other school at which the student intends to enroll.

Earlier, the House of Representatives had rejected a similar proposal, but the Buckley amendment survived the work of a conference committee and, on July 31, 1974, the House reversed itself and approved the provision. In his first address to Congress, President Ford pledged to sign it into law.

The mere existence of laws and rules, of course, does not guarantee they will be observed. A principal told Diane Divoky,

"I know what the law is here in California. Parents are supposed to be able to see the cumulative record. But if a parent comes in and asks to see a record, first I ask why. If there's a really good reason, I'll share some of it with them—but there are certain items I'll always withhold."

The difficulty parents face in getting access to their childrens' records is more than matched by the difficulty in keeping un-authorized persons out of the files. A group of parents sued to prevent the House of Representatives District of Columbia Com-mittee from circulating its report on District schools that iden-tified a large number of school children by name as "class-cut-ters," "disruptive," or "anti-social." The government assured the courts, including the United States Supreme Court, that there would be no further distribution of the report. Nevertheless, a year after those assurances were made, a member of the ACLU staff got a copy by the simple expedient of asking for it from the House Document Room in the Capitol.

The ultimate consequences of a school's concern with the "whole child" show up in a program known as the "Magic Circle" recently introduced into six public schools in Pittsburgh, Pennsylvania. Developed some years earlier by Harold Bessell and Uvaldo Palomares of the Human Development Training Institute in El Cajon, California, and previously adopted by some Califor-nia schools, the "Magic Circle" is one of a number of "affective education" programs now under consideration across the country. These programs are supposed to be "preventive mental health measures" for children. They are intended to increase teachers' "empathy" and improve their ability to "relate" to students. Availability of federal funds under Title III of the Elementary and Secondary Education Act makes them even more popular. Costs and salary increments to teachers who take part in a couple of weekend retreats set up to train leaders for "Magic Circles" can be covered by the government. The Pittsburgh project cost $51,260 in its first year, a similar amount the second year.

Here is how the "Magic Circle" works in Pittsburgh: eight to twelve students and a teacher meet at least twice a week for twenty to thirty minutes at a time. They sit in a circle. The leader, at first the teacher, brings up a topic known as the "cue." Typical "cues" include, "Having nice feelings and bad feelings, too," "Something that made me feel bad," "Somebody got me into trouble," and "How I got somebody to pay attention to me." Any child who wants to speak gets a turn. The leader focuses on emotions ("How did you feel about it?"). All actions and feelings are accepted as okay; nothing is labeled as good or bad, even if the child reports dropping a cat out of the window or stealing a bicycle. Participants are encouraged to paraphrase each other's contributions (known as "reflecting"). "Debriefing," follows on such subjects as "How I knew that someone was listening to me," "Something new I learned about myself," "Something new I learned about another," and "Why I enjoy the sessions."

The basic lesson taught in the "Magic Circle" is that nothing should be kept to yourself. Disclose all to everybody, and you'll feel better for it. When Roman Catholics go to confession, they tell their sins to one person who is bound by both canon law and civil law to absolute silence about what he has heard. There is no such privacy in the "Magic Circle." A parent whose children participated in the "Magic Circle" in the Castro School in Mt. View, California, wrote, "I believe our first knowledge of its use was at the dinner table when we, as a family, usually talk over the day's happenings. It seemed our children were beginning to relate to us as much information regarding other families ... perhaps details which they ordinarily would not know, from families of children with whom they had little acquaintance."

Participation in the "Magic Circle" is supposed to be voluntary, yet, the manual encourages group pressure: "In an interpersonal environment characterized by respect members will feel secure and will risk self-disclosure to gain acceptance." If members are silent, the teacher is told to "establish eye contact with certain members and/or extend an open invitation to take one's turn in the session." The manual instructs teachers to "indicate your appreciation of the children who volunteered. Discuss how brave these children are and how lucky to find out what other people find objectionable about them."

Along the way, the "Magic Circle" churns up information for school dossiers on students and teachers. In its first year in Pittsburgh, something called the "California Personality Inventory" was used to test teachers and measure changes in their ability to "empathize." The second year it was replaced by a test to measure "Attitude Toward Teaching as a Career." Teachers (or "Group Facilitators" as this questionnaire labels them) must complete an "Interpersonal Relationship Rating Scale" on the children, rating them on such matters as "Tendency to seek close personal relationships with others," "Degree of peace of mind," and "Willingness to discuss feelings and emotions with others." It is not clear what, if any, limitations there are supposed to be on such gossip, or on the circulation of such private information.

School dossiers are compiled very casually. Why not? Schools are benevolent institutions. They have no adversary relationship with their students. That, at any rate, is the theory for including observations about the "whole child" in school records. In practice, the derogatory comments inserted in the records so casually by teachers, guidance counselors, and principals transform them into the adversaries of the child. And, it is an unequal contest. Schools start the process by labeling some children as bad. Once started, the process may never end.

2

Is Your Child a "Special" Child?
ABILITY-GROUPING DOSSIERS

Donald Nicoletti, Jr., had a reading deficiency, or so his parents, Donald and Jacqueline Nicoletti of Closter, New Jersey, were told by Hillside Elementary School. Donald Jr. was placed in a "small class" to help him overcome his problem. He would return to a regular fourth-grade class after six months.

The Nicolettis soon became aware the "small class" was for "special education"; the children in it were segregated from the rest of the children at Hillside; they had lunch and physical education with a mentally retarded class; and they went to and from school in special school buses. Donald Jr.'s reading did not improve in the "small class," and he seemed to regress in other subjects, such as mathematics. Worst of all, he was considered mentally retarded by his friends because he was segregated from their classes and activities.

Deciding that their son must have been put into this "special class" as a result of special tests by the school, Donald and Jacqueline Nicoletti asked to see the records. They were turned down. The following summer, they were informed that Donald Jr. had been assigned to another "small class," for the school year ahead. The Nicolettis took Donald Jr. to a private specialist, who tested him and reported there was no basis for putting him in a special education class. Nevertheless, a school official insisted that Donald Jr.'s placement in a class for the neurologically impaired was "consistent with the records available." The parents were again denied the right to see the records.

In desperation, the Nicolettis took Donald Jr. out of Hillside. They attempted to enroll him in several Roman Catholic schools in the area. Each application was rejected, apparently on the basis of information furnished by Hillside. Finally, they succeeded in enrolling him in a private nondenominational school at a tuition cost of $1250 for the school year. Donald Jr. did well and, on the strength of that record, was accepted in a Roman Catholic school for the next school year. He took a normal course of studies and got mostly Bs—except for reading. In that he got an A.

A label like "mentally retarded" is one of the hazards of attending public school. The consequences of such a label may mean exclusion from public school, or it may mean placement in a "special education" class, often just "a euphemism for a day-sitting room staffed by an unqualified teacher." [1] Infrequently, "special education" classes give extra attention to the children in them, though often without demonstrable benefit. Even in the best programs, the quality of instruction does not compensate children for the damage done by the sense of shame they suffer.

The "mentally retarded" label is a special hazard for children of poor and, therefore, of minority group families. They do not have the option of fighting back by arranging for their children to be privately tested, or by paying $1250 for tuition at a private school as the Nicolletis were able to do.

A recent study [2] found schools, more than any other institution, excelled in labeling individuals as mentally retarded and distribut-

1. David Kirp, "Student Classification, Public Policy, and the Courts," *Harvard Educational Review* 44, no. 1 (February 1974): 19.

2. Jane R. Mercer, *Labelling the Mentally Retarded* (Berkeley: University of California Press, 1972).

ing the information widely. In Riverside, California, the focus of the study, 81 percent of the public school children are white or Anglo, 11 percent are Mexican-Americans, and 8 percent are black. These figures fairly closely corresponded to the number of children of each racial group selected by their teachers for testing to determine if they were mentally retarded, but a racial imbalance appeared after IQ tests were administered. On the strength of the tests, 32.1 percent of those stigmatized as mentally retarded were Anglos, 45.3 percent were Mexican-Americans, and 22.6 percent were blacks. The study blamed the racial disproportions on "Anglocentrism" in the IQ tests. Lack of training in the English language and lack of familiarity with the history, traditions, and institutions of the majority culture depressed test scores.

In the New York City public schools, about 10,000 children are consigned to CRMD classes. CRMD stands for Children with Retarded Mental Development. The curriculum they get in elementary school is usually limited to such instruction as toilet habits, the value of milk as food, the danger of eating between meals, and the appropriate clothes for different occasions. Little instruction is offered in reading, spelling, and arithmetic. When CRMD children are fourteen, they are promoted from toilet training and such subjects to vocational training in limited trades like cleaning, pressing, laundering, and food handling.

Children are placed in CRMD classes on the basis of their performance on the Wechsler Intelligence Scale for Children (WISC). The WISC test, constructed in 1950 by testing 2,200 persons, all white, is valid only for whites, according to the test's author, David Wechsler. It has undergone no significant revisions since 1950 and is administered only in English. Although the staff instructions of the New York City Board of Education and the regulations of the commissioner of education of the State of New York caution against exclusive reliance on intelligence tests of the WISC variety, in practice, the tests alone usually determine which children are committed to CRMD classes. Puerto Rican and black children are placed in these classes about twice as often as their proportion of the school population would seem to warrant.

A few years ago, forty-seven Mexican-American children in California in classes for the educable mentally retarded took new IQ tests administered in Spanish. The unsurprising result was that their IQs went up, from an average of 70 on the English language test to 83 on the Spanish language test. The results of the Spanish language test would have placed only ten of these children—not 47—in the educable mentally retarded category.

Such studies have stimulated several court decisions which strike down traditional methods of classifying children as mentally retarded. A 1970 California case, *Diane v. State Board of Education*, requires Spanish-speaking children to be tested in Spanish and insists on the development of a non–culturally biased IQ test. All Mexican-American and Chinese children already in classes for the educable retarded must be retested. The courts reached similar results in Arizona and Louisiana. Every child who is educable, no matter how severe his retardation or handicap, the courts also say is entitled to an education geared to his circumstances; none can be excluded.

The California, Arizona, and Louisiana court decisions protect a child who is to be classified by compelling schools to follow procedures designed to insure that decisions are fair. Notice of the reasons for classification must be sent to the parents; the child has the right to a hearing before a hearing officer; parents must be notified of their right to receive independent medical, psychological, and educational evaluation at no cost; children and parents have a right to free counsel. Most important of all, the parents and their counsel can examine all records before the hearing, and all tests or reports on which the action is based. They may confront and cross-examine the persons who made out the reports.

Despite such progress, thousands of children are excluded from school altogether because they are classified in their dossiers as mentally or physically handicapped. The U.S. Office of Education estimates a million or so are excluded from school. When

Peter Mills was in the fourth grade at the Brent Elementary School, he was thrown out of school as a "behavior problem," expelled without a hearing. Along with other black children from broken homes in Washington, D.C., Peter now lives in Junior Village totally separated from publicly supported education.

Duane Blacksheare, also black, was thrown out of the Giddings Elementary School when he was in third grade, also a behavior problem and also without a hearing or periodic review of his status. For the next four years, Duane Blacksheare did not attend school at all. Then he was tested by the Child Study Center in Washington, D.C.: the Center said he could return to school if he had help—"supportive services." He was put back in a regular seventh-grade class without any catch-up assistance, had trouble keeping up with children who had been in school the four years he was out, and, as a result, was again excluded. He and Peter Mills are plaintiffs in *Mills v. Board of Education of the District of Columbia,* a landmark case which is forcing school systems to stop excluding children so casually and in such great numbers.

The case for turning such troublesome children away from the public schools has frequently been advocated by Albert Shanker, now president of the American Federation of Teachers and, even when he only headed the New York City United Federation of Teachers, the most powerful spokesman for teachers nationally. "The student whose aberrant behavior consumes most of the teacher's time and energy" is, says Shanker, what "many teachers consider the number one problem." In one of a series of weekly advertisements camouflaged as columns, inserted by the U.F.T. at the cost of more than $100,000 a year each Sunday on the education page of the *New York Times,* Shanker reprinted an article by Hyman Eigerman which argued that exclusion of "maladjusted children was a way of upholding children's rights. . . . Of all the ways by which our children's right to learn is violated, the single most damaging one in my opinion, is the insistence on keeping severely maladjusted children in the common school. They pre-

sent chronic and, so far as the capacities of the school are concerned, incorrigible behavior problems that initiate and promote
massive disruption of the classroom."

If the Albert Shankers have their way, the number of children
consigned to special classes, special schools, and, perhaps, no
schools, will multiply. Court decisions protecting the right to
education will be hard to implement if organized teacher power
takes an adversary position.

A less drastic, but even more pervasive, form of labeling children, with the overwhelming support of teachers, is "ability
grouping" or "tracking." Starting as early as the first grade, children are tested and otherwise evaluated and placed on a track
reflecting the school's estimate of their intellectual ability. The
track will determine a child's friends and associates, the pace and
level of instruction he will receive, and the kinds of courses open
to him.

Once on a particular track, it is not easy for a child to get off. A
child on a slow track in elementary school can seldom demonstrate the academic achievement he will need in high school to get
on a track headed for college. Tracking decisions made in the
earliest years of school crucially affect a child's life possibilities;
yet these vital decisions depend on such haphazardly reliable
measuring devices as IQ tests, early grades, and the observations
of teachers and guidance counselors. The dossier-mongers find a
ripe harvest.

A 1959 survey by the National Education Association found
that 77.5 percent of school districts with more than 2,500 pupils
were using ability grouping in the elementary grades, 90.5 percent in high school. A 1967 follow-up study by the NEA said little
had changed.

Tracking allows bright and intelligent children to go fast and
other children to go at their own pace. At least, so the theory goes.
Everyone benefits. Despite the popularity of grouping, there is
little evidence on its educational consequences. Some of the evi-

dence which does exist is contradictory. Probably the most one can say is that the process appears of slight if any advantage to children on a fast track and somewhat more *dis*advantageous to children on a slow track. The classmates of children on a slow track are excluded from contact with other children who might stimulate them to achieve; perhaps of greater significance, these children come to conform to lower teacher expectations. Then dossiers predict—and encourage—failure.

Harvard psychologist Robert Rosenthal conducted an experiment in a California school. Young children were given an intelligence test and their teachers were told that the tests of 20 percent of the children selected at random showed that they could be expected to do especially well in school during the year ahead. Some had indeed excelled on the tests, but some had actually done very poorly. They came, incidentally, from families of very varied social and economic status.

The following year all the children took intelligence tests again. Remarkable gains were registered only by the group of children the teachers were told would make such gains. In some cases, these randomly selected children improved their scores by twenty or twenty-five points. The behavior of the children designated in advance as "spurters" by the teachers also improved.[3]

Tracking has large social consequences, as well. My son attended a public school in Manhattan, superficially something of a model of racial integration. The school population is roughly one third white, one third black, and one third Puerto Rican. Except, it isn't that way in class. The school was tracked, and the white children were bunched in fast tracks. Whatever predispositions the various racial groups had to associate with their own kind were effectively reinforced, as were their stereotyped perceptions of each other.[4]

3. Robert Rosenthal and Lenore Jacobson, *Pygmalion in the Classroom* (New York: Holt, Rinehart & Winston, 1968).
4. The school did make one concession to the idea of mixing children from different backgrounds; social studies classes were not tracked, apparently in the belief that in this subject it would be desirable to allow the children to study each other.

Assignment to a slow track may not produce a sense of shame in children comparable to the label of mentally retarded, but it is painfully stigmatizing, all the same. David Kirp has written in the *Harvard Educational Review*, "The effects of school-imposed stigmas do not ease when the child leaves school, for schools are society's most active labelers. Slow track assignment makes college entrance nearly impossible and may discourage employers from offerings jobs." [5] Whatever the few inhibitions schools maintain against giving outsiders anecdotal records, virtually no restraints are enforced on the release of academic records.

Ability grouping also implies, as individuals like Shockley and Jensen would have it, that intelligence is hereditary rather than environmental. By assigning a child to a slow track, the school makes the record the child acquires in his earliest days at school an immutable guide to his life. No stimulus provided by the school can be expected to promote him upward. The school aids the child in filling the niche for which he has already been destined. Tracking thus is in conflict with the idea that school is a place in which a child's horizons can be expanded. It is in conflict with a democratic society.

In greatly disproportionate numbers, members of racial minorities are consigned to slow tracks or "special education" classes, or excluded from school entirely. These devices maintain segregation in ostensibly integrated schools. Their impact is often far more devastating than the explicit segregation outlawed by the U.S. Supreme Court in the 1954 *Brown* decision. A "special" child, in such programs is a rejected child.

5. Op. cit. p. 23

3

"Did Your Parents Hug and Kiss You Good Night?"

PREDELINQUENCY PREDICTIONS

Juanita has problems relating properly to one of her sisters. She is not working at grade level in reading and math. She lacks motivation, has a short span of interest, demonstrates an inability to have fun and is withdrawn.

She also steals pencils and other items from other children.

This harsh judgment of a nine-year-old's behavior rendered by a teacher at the Glenknoll Drive Elementary School in Yorba Linda, California, sent that child to a federally funded program for "predelinquents."

The program is called VISA, which stands for Volunteers Influencing Student Achievement. A California legislative audit describes how children get into VISA:

The children in the program are initially referred to the program by a teacher who has made a determination that the program can help. A child may be referred for either behavioral or academic problems, but there are no established criteria defining the type of behavior or academic problem which will be referred. One of the goals of the program is to define the types of problems which lead to delinquency.

In its first year of operation, 137 children from grades one to six were referred to the program as "predelinquents." Adult counselors were assigned to them.

VISA is, of course, intended to benefit the children referred to it. Perhaps it does, perhaps not. What is certain is that it creates a lot of files. A monthly report is made out on each child in the program. These reports are stored in the offices of SMILE (which stands for Something Meaningful in Local Effort), the Orange County Probation Department's community service project in the town of Placentia. Copies go to a University of Southern California research institute that is studying VISA.

There are no provisions for destruction of the record of Juanita's referral to VISA or of the monthly reports on her performance in the program. As the California legislative audit stated:

The pre-delinquent programs are essentially pilot projects, one of the purposes of which is to validate certain hypotheses on delinquency prediction and prevention. As pilot projects, any residual records after termination of the project should relate only to proving or disproving of the concepts sought to be proven or disproven.

Accordingly, there is no need for individual records being maintained. In fact, the existence of individual records long after their need has passed presents the real possibility that such records will be used for purposes other than that for which they were accumulated.

Spotting Juanita as a potential criminal because she doesn't have fun and takes pencils costs a lot of money. The money comes from the Orange County Probation Department, which in turn, gets its funds from the California Council on Criminal Justice (CCCJ), the state agency established to obtain and administer grants from the federal government's Law Enforcement Assistance Administration (LEAA). In fiscal 1972, LEAA spent about $700 million to help states strengthen law enforcement. About 14 percent, or $58,919,841, went for prevention and control of juvenile delinquency. Part of that money went into spotting Juanita as a predelinquent and treating her accordingly. The Nixon administration was so delighted with LEAA that, in a year when other federal programs were drastically cut, LEAA was authorized to spend $1.75 billion in fiscal 1973.[1]

LEAA's genealogy is rooted in the liberal reformist impulse. In 1967, the President's Commission on Law Enforcement issued its, in some ways, admirable report, "The Challenge of Crime in a Free Society." One of its less happy consequences was its view of the bureaucracies—prosecutorial, defense, judicial, prison, probation, and parole—that are concerned with crimes. They were seen as a single "criminal justice system." It probably *is* a system, but accurate or not, it was an unfortunate perception. Good government instincts being what they are, the best public officials promptly set about to make that "system" more systematic.

The President's Commission on Law Enforcement published its report just about the time Ramsey Clark became acting attorney general; it gave strong support to his view that there was an urgent need to improve the performance of local police. It was a time when summer riots were endemic in major American cities, often touched off by brutality or racial slurs by police.

A modestly funded program of grants to local police agencies, the Federal Law Enforcement Assistance Act of 1965, produced some useful results. Clark's book *Crime in America* describes in glowing terms one of its projects, a Family Crisis Intervention Unit of eighteen police officers in a precinct in Manhattan's Upper West Side. In the hope of funding comparably humane and intelligent police programs nationwide, Clark proposed expansion of federal aid to local criminal justice agencies.

1. On August 15, 1974, Senate-House conferees agreed on a bill to further expand federal programs to combat juvenile delinquency. Over and above the $140 million already allocated to juvenile delinquency by LEAA in fiscal 1974, the conference committee bill would authorize appropriations of an additional $75 million in 1974, $125 million in 1975, and $150 million in 1976. All this money would be under the control of a new Office of Juvenile Justice and Delinquency Prevention within LEAA. With all that money to spend, it ought to be possible to identify and treat a lot of "predelinquents."

The result was the Safe Streets and Crime Control Act of 1967, greeted with loud applause from liberal and libertarian spokesmen, including this writer. Unfortunately, several funny things happened to the 1967 act on its way to expansion as the Safe Streets and Crime Control Act of 1968. The law came to sanction wiretapping, despite Attorney General Clark's adamant opposition. In addition, the state governments successfully intruded into the administration of all federal grants that supported local law enforcement programs. Congress was taking pains to insure that Ramsey Clark's own notions of criminal justice would not be fostered by the grants.

The vast sums of money presently being spent by LEAA have helped many police departments acquire stocks of hardware which would be the envy of the armies of many foreign countries. They have paid for helicopters, electronic command and control equipment, television cameras and monitors for street surveillance, vehicle locators, and night sensors. Much of this equipment was originally designed for use in the Vietnam war. The same business corporations that found war lucrative are turning handsome profits out of LEAA's war on crime.

LEAA is a prime supporter of the collection of data on individuals who have committed crimes, or are alleged to have committed crimes, or who *might* commit crimes some time in the future. The most publicized LEAA grants have supported computerized systems; however, some LEAA funded data collection programs, like VISA, are much more primitive. For its work in identifying Juanita and 136 other young children as predelinquents, maintaining records on them, and treating them as predelinquents, VISA got $119,866 for two years' work, a modest sum compared to LEAA's grants for computerized information systems.

LEAA is rather sensitive about its funding of programs for "predelinquents." The very term suggests the products of the "Social Predestination Room" in Aldous Huxley's *Brave New World*. In the spring of 1973 when a syndicated news story said that young children in California were being identified as predelinquents, fingerprinted, and their names filed in computers, the LEAA administrator, Donald Santarelli, counterattacked in a letter to Marian Wright Edelman, director of the Children's Defense Fund. "LEAA is not involved in any program whereby kindergarten and lower-grade children are being identified as predelinquent and their names filed in a computer, or in any program whereby teachers are being asked to identify such children," Santarelli wrote on July 10, 1973. "The projects [LEAA financed] have nothing to do with fingerprinting children and putting information about them into computers. The purpose of the projects is the prevention of and control of juvenile delinquency. The programs deal almost exclusively with teenagers. In no cases are kindergarten children involved. In fact, the programs have nothing to do with the schools. They are run by the county probation departments."

In charity to Santarelli, one assumes he could not have known about the VISA program. The young children in that program are referred by teachers. LEAA also funded, through the California Council on Criminal Justice, Operation Early Success at the Lakeshore Elementary School in Foster City, California.

A program for children in kindergarten and early primary grades, Operation Early Success was "intended to reduce trends toward delinquency within the county." University of California researchers would track children identified as predelinquents to determine how many ended up in prison. The program was discontinued on June 30, 1972, but the records of those children identified for inclusion in the program went into their cumulative school records. Some of the children are still being traced by the University of California researchers.

Another California predelinquent identification program similar to VISA is known by euphemistic camouflage as Alternate Routes. More than 1,600 children were placed in the Alternate Routes program in its first sixteen months. "Right now, any teacher can refer any child to a program for any reason," said James C. Bassett, an attorney who led a state inquiry into the Orange County program, in an interview with the *Los Angeles Times.* "It could be just the gut reaction of a teacher to a child. We found one child was referred to a program on the second day of kindergarten."

In these matters, California is usually out ahead of the rest of the country. Other states are trying to catch up.

A program known as Critical Period of Intervention (CPI) was scheduled to start in Montgomery County, Pennsylvania, in October 1972. Its purpose was to identify potential drug users. The arrival of CPI was heralded with a letter to parents. CPI proposed to have psychological questionnaires filled out by children and their teachers. The children were to be asked such questions as:

Which of these four students is most like you?
1) Someone who will probably be a success in life.
2) One who gets upset when faced with a difficult school problem.
3) Someone who has lots of self-confidence.
4) A student who has more problems than other students.

The child was to tell whether his parents "hugged and kissed me good night when I was small" or "tell me how much they love me." Teachers were asked to identify which child in class could best be characterized by this statement: "This pupil makes unusual or inappropriate responses during normal school activities. His behavior is unpredictable."

Ms. Sylvia Merriken of Norristown was one of the parents who received a letter about the program. She complained about it to Stewart Junior High School and to the Norristown School Board. When that didn't work she sought the help of the ACLU of Pennsylvania and brought suit. On September 28, 1973, Federal District Judge Morgan Davis ordered a stop to the CPI program.

In his decision, Judge Davis noted that, in addition to requiring answers to questions of the "hugged and kissed me" variety, the CPI questionnaires asked both students and teachers "to identify other students in the class who make unusual or odd remarks, get into fights or quarrels with other students, make unusual or inappropriate responses during normal school activities, or have to be coaxed or forced to work with other pupils. Students are at no time given any guidance as to what should be considered an odd or unusual remark or what is to be considered an inappropriate response. For example, there is no warning that political differences or unusual or imaginative insights should not be looked upon as odd remarks or inappropriate responses."

The initial letter to parents about CPI said: "We ask your support and cooperation in this program and assure you of the confidentiality of these studies." Judge Davis found this deceptive. "The CPI program," he wrote, "contemplates the development and distribution of the information obtained from the tests" to various school personnel, including superintendents, principals, guidance counselors, athletic coaches, social workers, PTA officers, and school board members. "Additionally, there is no assurance that the information would be immune to the subpoena power of law enforcement officials."

Two child psychiatrists testified at the trial. Judge Davis summarized their views in his decision, noting the "risk that the CPI Program will operate as a self-fulfilling prophecy in which a child labeled as a potential drug abuser will by virtue of a label decide to be that which people already think he or she is anyway. . . . Another danger mentioned is that of scapegoating in which a child might be marked out by his peers for unpleasant treatment either because of refusal to take the CPI test or because of the result of the test."

The decision by Judge Davis forbidding the Norristown School Board to run CPI is the first of its kind. Whether it will be followed by other courts remains to be seen.

In the meantime, many other predelinquent identification programs are going forward. Baltimore has a project known as Early Identification and Treatment of Delinquent Behavior, administered by the city school system and funded by the Governor's Commission on Law Enforcement and the Administration of Justice. Again, the money ultimately comes from LEAA. The project is attempting to develop tests to identify "maladaptive," "dangerous," or "potentially delinquent children." Tests which would classify children in this way had been given to about 10 percent of the children in Baltimore elementary schools in early 1974. The *Baltimore Sun* quoted project researchers as saying that a "50 percent accuracy rate" would be tolerated in predicting delinquency. If the people administering the tests get enough money, all the city's school children would be tested and classified. They are seeking $2,400,000 to finish the job.

A few years ago, another Maryland project for identifying children as potential criminals created a small furor. Under a research project funded by the National Institutes of Health, a federal government agency, blood samples were drawn from 15,000 Maryland boys for tests to discover whether they had XYY chromosomes.

Sex is determined by chromosome makeup. Women have an XX and most men have an XY chromosome. The theory that an XYY chromosome causes violent criminal behavior stems from the finding in some studies that such chromosomes are present in a disproportionately large number of inmates of prisons and mental hospitals. No cause and effect relationship has been established, but some geneticists speculate that the extra Y factor in the chromosome signifies extra masculinity and, therefore, extra aggressiveness.

Among those tested were 6,000 boys confined in the state's juvenile jails, many incarcerated simply because they are neglected children, not because they have committed crimes. Others tested included some 7,500 East Baltimore boys, almost all of them black and poor, who are enrolled in free child care programs at Johns Hopkins. The results of the tests were to be available to juvenile correctional agencies.

The project attracted attention because of a series of articles about it in 1970 by Diane Bauer in the *Washington Daily News.* Robert C. Hilson, director of Juvenile Services for Maryland, told Ms. Bauer the blood test results stigmatizing the boys for life as potential criminals, "will probably be passed on to the courts for whatever use they can make of it."

The news stories aroused a small controversy over Johns Hopkins University's exploitation of poor children who were receiving free medical care as research subjects. No permission had been sought from the boys' parents or guardians because Johns Hopkins routinely tested blood for anemia, and simply used the same sample to test for XYY chromosomes. Five hundred boys in a private psychiatric hospital, Edgemeade, were also tested without any special permission from parents. Parents of children at Edgemeade had signed blanket permission forms when their children were admitted to the institution.

Consent was sought from the parents or guardians of the 6,000 boys confined in juvenile institutions, many confined because their parents neglected them. The covering letter and consent form were less than informative. The covering letter read:

Your son, who is presently at _____, has been included in a special diagnostic genetic (chromosome) study. This test is being conducted with the administrative approval of the Director, Department of Juvenile Services, State of Maryland, Baltimore, Maryland. We plan to test 6,000 boys in a period of three years, from all the state institutions.

Please sign the enclosed form and mail it in the enclosed stamped, addressed envelope at your earliest convenience.

The consent form enclosed read:

Date: _____

Boy's Name: _____

As his parents and/or legal guardian, I give permission for a blood sample to be drawn from the above named youngster for examination by the staff of the Division of Medical Genetics of this institution.

It is understood that no drugs or medication will be administered; that the results of the examination will be made known to me upon request; and that there will be no charge for this service.

_____

Signature of parent(s) or
legal guardian

Probation officers were recruited to persuade recalcitrant parents to sign the consent forms.

Diane Bauer's news accounts and an ACLU lawsuit forced a temporary halt in the blood testing. Testing was resumed when authorities produced a more explicit consent form. Parents of boys already tested were not told that their children's rights might have been violated or that new consent forms had been prepared.

The credit for the idea of testing children to determine if they are likely to become delinquents goes primarily to Harvard sociologists Sheldon and Eleanor Glueck. They developed a series of criteria for predicting delinquency and urged "timely clinical and social intervention, which gives the greatest promise of redirecting the endangered child." [2]

The most sweeping proposal for predelinquency testing came from Dr. Arnold Hutschneker, a former personal physician of President Richard Nixon. Hutschneker wrote a 1,600-word memorandum to the president as a critique of the work of the National Commission on the Causes and Prevention of Violence. As such bodies will do, the commission, established in the wake of the assassinations of Martin Luther King, Jr., and Robert F. Kennedy,

2. Sheldon and Eleanor Glueck, *Predicting Delinquency and Crime* (Cambridge, Mass.: Harvard University Press, 1960), p. 16.

had called for restructuring the social environment. "No doubt there is a desperate need for the urban reconstruction," Hutschneker wrote to Nixon. "But I would suggest another, direct, immediate and I believe effective way of tackling the problem at its very origin, by focusing on the criminal mind of the child. The government should have mass testing on all 6-to-8-year-old children to help detect the children who have violent and homicidal tendencies. Corrective treatment could begin at that time."

There are more than 12½ million six, seven, and eight-year-olds in the country. Hutschneker proposed to test them all for "violent and homicidal tendencies" through such devices as Rorschach ink blots.

President Nixon was apparently impressed. Hutschneker's proposal was forwarded to the Department of Health, Education and Welfare by a White House aide with a covering letter saying, "the President asks your opinion as to the advisability of setting up pilot projects embodying some of these approaches."

The Hutschneker proposal and the president's interest in it prompted the American Psychological Association, the American Sociological Association, and the American Psychiatric Association to hold a joint press conference of protest. Speaking for the American Psychological Association on April 10, 1973, Dr. Kenneth B. Little said, "Dr. Hutschneker shows a complete lack of understanding as to what psychological tests can or cannot do or even what they are meant to do." Noting the likelihood of 50 percent errors, Dr. Little said, "The damage to the child and the family of erroneous classification is not possible to estimate." Dr. Edmund H. Volkart, speaking for the American Sociological Association at the same press conference, said, "The notion that anyone knows what 'the criminal mind' is in a 6-year-old is absurd. Deviancy doesn't necessarily mean crime or delinquency. It can also mean some damn fresh, new ideas about the world. These tests can't distinguish. If Michelangelo had been tested at age 6, they'd probably have killed him."

Of course, Dr. Hutschneker never recommended killing any-one. His proposal for children shown by the tests to be severely disturbed was only that they be put away in special camps.

Despite the disparaging views of the country's leading associations of psychologists, psychiatrists, and sociologists, the "pilot projects" sought by former President Nixon embodying Dr. Hutschneker's proposals appear to be going forward. It remains to be seen if his successor will halt this dangerous program. If the proponents of these proposals are right, they will accurately predict delinquency. If the critics are right, the identification and treatment of children as predelinquents will be a self-fulfilling prophecy; children will become delinquents because society expects them to be. Either way, it seems likely the pilot projects will produce results supporting their extension.

4

Pitching Pennies, Throwing Snowballs, and Using Profane Language
JUVENILE COURT DOSSIERS

Walter Weisberg is a diabetic. One day in a Lynbrook, Long Island, grocery store, he had a diabetic seizure. He grabbed something sweet to eat and, as a result, found himself under arrest. When the reasons for his "theft" became known, the charges were dropped.

That should have been the end of the matter. After all, Weisberg was a teen-ager at the time, and New York has strict laws against the disclosure of juvenile arrest records. Section 784 of New York's Family Court Act says, "All police records relating to the arrest and disposition of any person under this article shall be kept in files separate and apart from the arrests of adults and shall be withheld from public inspection."

Nevertheless, Weisberg brought suit to have the record of his arrest destroyed, and with good cause. Although juvenile arrest and disposition records are made confidential by the laws of twenty-three states, they circulate freely.

Weisberg lost. Five years later, in 1970, in a precedent-setting decision in another case, New York City Family Judge Nanette Dembitz ordered the expungement of the records of a fourteen-year-old and a fifteen-year-old arrested during a demonstration. Judge Dembitz said it was likely that employers would gain access to arrest records, and, therefore, expungement was necessary.

Even ordering the record wiped out might not work. Courts like the New York Family Court have no authority to order destruction of records forwarded elsewhere, as to the FBI or the army. A 1972 study by the Georgetown University Law School told of a child in California who got a court order expunging his arrest record. When he applied for a job with a private business, he denied ever having been arrested. California law has a specific provision allowing such denials. The employer got hold of the "sealed" record anyway and fired him for lying.

Twenty years ago, Alfred J. Kahn, in a study of the New York City Children's Court, found that the laws about the confidentiality of juvenile court records had not kept these records out of the hands of the FBI, Civil Service Commissions, the army, the Red Cross, the Hack License Bureau, the Department of Public Welfare, the Travelers Aid Society, and a variety of social agencies. A 1970 study by Alan Sussman found the situation unchanged, and, in 1971, a top FBI official, Beverly E. Ponder, director of the Bureau's Identification Division, testified in a trial that the FBI treated juvenile records exactly in the same manner as adult records. That is, they were freely disseminated.

Ironically, specialized courts for children were set up to avoid the stigmatization of criminal labeling—to keep the child from a public reputation that he is "bad" or "can't make it." As a consequence, most children's courts are closed to the press and the public. Lack of public scrutiny has led to shocking abuses. Arguments in favor of greater visibility for juvenile court proceedings have given way before the claims of privacy. The trade-off may have been a bad one because privacy has not been maintained. The arrest and disposition records of children are "confidential" in name only.

Juvenile probation officers spend almost a third of their time making out dossiers. A California legislative committee found that bureaucracies prepare more than one hundred documents recording the name of an arrested child. At least in theory, all these records should make for intelligent individual treatment of each child in trouble. The sad truth is that the records seem to be filled out less for the good of the child and more for the convenience of the compilers, who thus demonstrate what they have been doing with their time. Whatever the reason, the proliferation of records does not encourage confidentiality.

Juvenile court records become available in many ways. The adult who was the child in trouble may have to sign a waiver of confidentiality to get a job—no waiver, no job, and, if it is signed, no confidentiality. Such waivers are routinely required by many public and private employers.

The United States Army compels all enlistees to sign a statement permitting access to juvenile records; the New York State Identification and Intelligence System, which has custody over all arrest and conviction records, maintains a Military Liaison office to make access to the records easy.[1] The other armed services are equally insistent about penetrating the confidentiality which supposedly protects juvenile records. A navy questionnaire demands that: "This question must be answered truthfully, regardless of any advice you may have received from any person in authority to the effect that you did not have to report a particular action in applying for employment or to enter the services." In the air force recruits must sign this statement: "I certify that the Recruiter has instructed me that the concealment of any police, court or juvenile records pertaining to me can result in a dishonorable discharge from the United States Air Force."

So much for laws making juvenile court records confidential! If

1. When this writer asked the then director of NYSIIS, Dr. Robert Gallati, about his agency's treatment of juvenile records, Gallati responded that he interpreted state law to make disposition records confidential, but not the records of underlying arrests.

the recruit should be foolish enough to follow the state law under which his arrest and court treatment took place and conceal his record, the military can usually get it from the court itself.

In his February 8, 1974, column, Jack Anderson brought to light an internal navy memorandum from a Captain John R. Brock, expressing pique at instances when the records were not available. The memo said, "The reluctance of civil authorities to release juvenile record information is impeding recruiter efforts in screening applicants to obtain high quality recruits." Anderson noted that he talked to a navy spokesman about the memo; it was explained that the information eventually turns up, and then juveniles who have failed to report it are discharged for "fraudulent enlistment." These fraudulent enlistments were estimated to be costing the navy about $2 million a year.

"Institutional and other non-governmental employers in the District of Columbia area routinely require job applicants to obtain and provide copies of their arrest records or 'police clearance,' " according to the Duncan Commission, an official District of Columbia body formed to investigate the dissemination of arrest records. In a single week in 1967, 3,672 arrest records were furnished this way. The commission said the deputy chief of police in charge of the Youth Aid Division told it that "a 'clearance' system, closely paralleling the system in effect with respect to adult offenders, is operated for the purpose of aiding [sic] juveniles in finding employment." Apparently, this practice was thought to be "aiding" juveniles get jobs because it eased the paths of those *without* records. It certainly didn't aid those *with* records. Rather laconically, the commission noted the provisions of the D.C. code making juvenile records confidential, and said the practice, "no matter how well intentioned, is clearly inappropriate."

As in the case of the schools, juvenile courts rely heavily on records of IQ tests. The family courts in New York City, like the schools in New York City, mostly depend on the Wechsler Intelligence Scale for Children to help them decide where to place neglected children or those who have broken the law. A child who scores below 70 is probably headed for an indefinite stay in an institution for the mentally retarded. If the score is over 70 but under 90 to 100, the placement will probably be in a state training school. A score over 100, and occasionally as low as 90, may get a child into a private institution, usually a preferable alternative.

Most children who come into the New York City family courts are black and Puerto Rican. Nevertheless, the critical decision on where to place children is based on a test its author never intended to be used on nonwhites. If the children are returned to the public schools, the test results follow them and help determine where they are allocated within the schools as well.

Juvenile records hold vast amounts of information based on unreviewed observations by police or probation officers. An example is the Y.D. card maintained by the New York City Police Department.

Y.D., which stands for Youth Division, cards, made out by police for many forms of minor legal infractions and for noncriminal behavior, are routinely issued, sometimes as an alternative to arresting a child, but often for conduct which could not be grounds for an arrest. A child police regard as a truant or a child charged with sneaking under a subway turnstile without paying the fare (known as a "Farebeat" in police manuals) is a typical candidate for a Y.D. card.

Eleven-year-old Michael Evans (not his real name) wanted to play a part in opposing the war in Vietnam. A demonstration against the war was scheduled that day in Central Park, and Michael felt he should be there. He lived in Queens, his parents couldn't take him, and he wasn't allowed to go on the subways by himself. So Michael organized a few friends to demonstrate against the war in the schoolyard.

Listening to television news reports about the Central Park demonstration, Michael and his friends heard that several hundred young men were planning to burn their draft cards there.

In an effort to share in that event, Michael and his friends pre-pared simulated draft cards which they burned in the schoolyard. A passing policeman collared Michael and gave him a Y.D. card for starting an "unauthorized fire." A few days later, the local police precinct called Michael's school to let them know about the Y.D. card. As a result, and despite a protest by the New York Civil Liberties Union, Michael lost his post as a member of the honor guard which carried the flag at school assemblies and as the fifth-grade reporter for the school newspaper.

There is no hearing or judicial scrutiny before or after a Y.D. card is issued. Concepts of due process—confrontation of accusers, cross-examination, right to remain silent, the right to present evidence and compel witnesses, counsel, presumption of innocence, proof beyond a reasonable doubt—are irrelevant. A police officer who has seen something himself or who has heard about an incident from someone who claims to be a witness, acts as prosecutor, judge, and jury and executes punishment.

Among the offenses that can be checked off on a Y.D. form are "Pitching Pennies," "Throwing Snowballs," "Using Profane Language," and "Smoking." Cards are also issued to children under sixteen who are present in bars, dance halls, bowling alleys, or billiard parlors. Truants frequently get Y.D. cards. Cards have even been issued for such offenses as dropping a gum wrapper on the floor of a subway train. A child who is a *victim* of sexual assault gets a card!

A New York City Criminal Justice Coordinating Council study of the 53,681 cards drawn by police in 1969 found that almost half were for "behavior which, exercising discretion differently, might not have been administratively acted upon." The study noted that the demeanor of a child was an important element in determining whether a card is issued. Observers for the study reported that: "regardless of the severity of the offense, a brash antagonistic, unrepentant, and, most important, disrespectful child was almost assured of receiving a card . . . a repentant attitude was the best assurance of avoiding one. . . ." Setting was important: "a less repentant attitude, or a more serious offense might be excused if the child were alone, but if the conduct occurred in the presence of others, officers felt obliged to take a strict approach." A child who thought he had rights and said so would be in worse trouble than a child who cringed before the police.

Precincts in New York City keep the Y.D. cards in their files. Copies are kept also in a central police department file. There are countywide files in suburban areas. Orange County, California, has what it calls a Central Juvenile Index. An accumulation of such cards makes a child a candidate for commitment to an institution as a "Person in Need of Supervision" (PINS). In New York State, police fill out about 2,000 petitions each year to get children institutionalized as PINS. In many more cases, police persuade someone else, family, school, or social agency, to petition to have children sent to PINS institutions. If a child should be involved in a family court proceeding, the information from the cards is made available to the probation officer assigned to the case. Police Department regulations let out information from the cards to a variety of public agencies including the Board of Education, Civil Service Commission, the armed services, Welfare Department, the district attorneys' offices, the Waterfront Commission, and the Port of New York Authority. Most of these agencies used the information to check on job seekers. Private social welfare agencies also get to see the cards.

A 1972 federal court case imposed some stricter limits on access to New York City Y.D. cards by people other than the police. It required destruction of the cards when the child reaches seventeen. In Philadelphia, such cards are destroyed at twenty-one. Still, the information could be kept alive in a family court record which would not be wiped out. On the basis of such information a child can be committed to an institution.

Most large police departments have some equivalent of the Y.D. card. Police argue that they help find runaways, identify gang members, and spot children who will later become involved in serious criminal acts. Filling out a card is thought to be a protection for children whose behavior might otherwise result in a formal arrest and criminal prosecution.

Few small towns bother with anything like Y.D. cards. Kids who get into trouble are personally known to the local constabulary. However, in small communities, as in large, the youngster who has been spotted as a "bad kid" may be regularly harassed or "rousted" by the police. "I have been picked up several times and questioned by the police," one young man told sociologist Edwin Lemert. "The police pulled me out of dances, saying I was drunk, even though I told them I don't drink. Finally, one day they blocked the street in front of my house and pulled me out on a marijuana charge . . . they try to make out that I'm part of a drug syndicate—imagine, here in Cowtown!" [2] If the police are rousting a young person, the town usually finds it out. To get a job, the person will probably have to leave town.

The small town victim of "rousting" does have one major advantage over his big city cousins. If he decides to move elsewhere to get away from his local fame, he may be able to do so successfully. Since the police in his home community know him on sight, they do not have to create a written record which might be accessible to employers and others in his refuge community. In the more impersonal world of the big city, a written record might track him wherever he runs.

During the course of any given year, about one million children are brought into juvenile court. Before age eighteen, one child in nine has a juvenile court record. Juvenile courts are supposed to help the 400,000 or so youngsters who are held to be law violators, or persons in need of supervision. In fact, those children are usually harmed rather than helped. Another 600,000 children are treated informally or have charges against them

2. In *On Record*, edited by Stanton Wheeler (New York: Russell Sage Foundation, 1969), p. 380.

dismissed. Police departments, juvenile courts, and other agencies keep dossiers of those court appearances just as they keep records of Y.D. cards or their local equivalents. And, laws to the contrary notwithstanding, they pass the information along to other groups.

An attorney experienced in defending children, Stephen Wizner, has described a conversation with a client after the successful conclusion of a case. It went like this:

"Did we win or lose?"

"We won."

"Yeah? What did we win?"

5

"The Walking Dead"

RECORDS OF TREATMENT FOR ADDICTION

"No reporting requirements are being met," said Governor Philip W. Noel of Rhode Island. "Therefore funds have been withheld." Sympatico, a "24-hour hot-line and drop-in center" in Wakefield, Rhode Island, would get no money to run a drug treatment program unless it gave the state information to identify patients. Many other drug treatment programs are running into similar problems.

The Department of Health of California ordered the closing of the five methadone maintenance programs in San Francisco in January 1974. At the time, more than 1,000 patients in San Francisco were enrolled in programs, many of them living relatively normal lives. They were swallowing methadone in orange juice once a day instead of injecting themselves two or three times a day with heroin (and, occasionally, hepatitis and other diseases). They were holding down steady jobs instead of shoplifting and burglarizing to pay their pushers.

The San Francisco clinics, backed by the city health department, had insisted that their patients' names be withheld from a statewide registry of methadone patients available to anyone with access to the data bank. San Francisco refused to allow the state any access to patients' records to permit individual identification.

The dispute broke open when Dr. Francis J. Curry, San Francisco's director of mental health, appended to his agreement to abide by various state regulations for operating methadone programs the comment: "Insofar as said statutes and regulations do not conflict or interfere with general law applicable to the confidential physician-patient relationship and records connected therewith. . . ."

California responded: "Since access to patient records is essential to adequate monitoring of such programs, this violation of regulations cannot be tolerated. State Authority approval for the operation of these methadone treatment programs will be denied."

Curry appealed. "Every patient record in the program will be made available to the inspection teams," he argued. "A comprehensive professional review of medical care and administrative practices can be done. . . . However . . . the names will be deleted from the patient record prior to your review so that patient-physician confidentiality will be maintained." That wasn't good enough for California, and the dispute has been taken into court.

Perhaps the most compelling case for disclosing the identity of patients arose in New York City. After Talmadge Berry was shot and killed in Manhattan on June 7, 1972, a witness told police she thought she had seen the killer in the waiting room of the methadone maintenance clinic at Francis Delafield Hospital, where she was also a patient. A grand jury ordered Dr. Robert Newman, director of the New York City Methadone Maintenance Treatment Program, to produce photographs of all Negro male patients between the ages of twenty-one and thirty-five. When Dr. Newman refused, he was held in contempt of court and sentenced to thirty days in jail. New York State's highest court, impressed by the arguments for maintaining the confidentiality of records of drug treatment, overturned the conviction.

Carl Beazer worked for the New York City Transit Authority for eleven years, moving up through competitive civil service exams from car cleaner to conductor to towerman. He was in a methadone program. He was fired by the Transit Authority when this fact was discovered.

Beazer had been a heroin addict all those eleven years. In April 1971, he voluntarily entered a Veterans Administration hospital to break his dependence. He had been on methadone only a few months when a physical examination on the job turned up methadone in his urine.

The Transit Authority is one of the largest employers in New York City. It provides more than 42,000 jobs, skilled, unskilled, or semiskilled. Rehabilitated drug addicts would appear to be eligible for many of them. Nevertheless, the Transit Authority has an absolute policy against employing participants in methadone programs.

New York has about 100,000 active heroin addicts, perhaps half of the country's total heroin population. The usual treatment is methadone. They may remain in the program for years and, if seriously addicted, for the rest of their lives. There is no known cure for heroin addiction. A maintenance program is often the addict's best chance for rehabilitation. That is, if he can get—and keep—a job.

In early 1974, the New York State Temporary Commission to Evaluate the Drug Laws issued a report on "Employing the Rehabilitated Addict." Several studies of methadone patients cited by the commission, including a long-term study of several thousand patients at Beth Israel and Bronx State Hospitals, showed that those who had been treated with methadone for five or six years were living almost completely normal lives. "As the period of observation in Methadone Maintenance Programs increases, the percent gainfully employed or occupied as homemakers increases to ninety-five percent and the proportion supported by welfare decreases to zero," the commission reported.

In New York City, about 32,000 addicts are enrolled in methadone maintenance programs, nationwide about 73,000. Three times that number could be brought into maintenance programs, but getting them in isn't easy. It is made much harder by job discrimination against those who try to help themselves.

The policies of the Transit Authority impede their efforts. So do the policies of Macy's, the New York Telephone Company, and the Western Electric Corporation, employers singled out by the New York State Commission in its report for their refusal to hire rehabilitated addicts.

The commission singled out for favorable mention employers like the First National City Bank and the Chase Manhattan Bank, who evaluated the work of rehabilitated addicts as indistinguishable from that of other employees. And, 150 men, working as truck drivers for employers who were unaware of their drug histories, were found by the commission "to perform well in jobs which are largely unsupervised, require good judgment and dexterity, offer temptations to behave unlawfully, and often present the dangers of fatigue and inattention. . . . This finding," said the commission, "should answer, once again, many of the objections of those who regard employment of rehabilitated addicts only from the standpoint of risk."

A Transit Authority spokesman, in response to the commission report in the *New York Times,* defended the refusal to hire methadone patients as "a policy dictated by an agency in a very critical business. . . . It would be sheer foolishness," he said, "to take any personnel risks where the safety of some six million daily riders might possibly be jeopardized." Apparently, it did not occur to the unnamed spokesman that those six million daily riders might be more jeopardized by desperate addicts not in the employ of the Transit Authority who are unable to find work or lead normal lives. They account for much of New York City's crime problem. The Transit Authority's business is getting people to business and pleasure safely and more or less on time. If people get mugged as they get off the bus or as they leave the subway station, that's someone else's problem, isn't it?

The Transit Authority's portrayal of itself as engaged "in a very critical business," and not willing to "take any personnel risks where the safety" of riders might be jeopardized might seem to some logical where addicts are concerned. Yet, the jobs that are absolutely barred to methadone patients include: car cleaner, collecting agent, light maintainer, maintainer's helper, railroad porter, turnstile maintainer, telephone maintainer, and ventilage and drainage maintainer. Surely, not all of these posts directly affect passenger safety. Nor is there evidence that individuals on methadone programs would endanger the public on other jobs.

The Transit Authority is not similarly antagonistic to alcoholics. They are not barred from employment. "Had Mr. Beazer been found drunk in the washroom or weaving along the tracks, what would have happened to him?" the New York commission asked. "He would have been referred for treatment. At the present time there are an estimated three thousand T.A. employees in treatment for alcoholism. Since Mr. Beazer had more than ten years of service with the T.A., if he had been an alcoholic, after he had dried out, he would have been returned to a less demanding job, but at *full pay.* . . . Moreover," the commission noted, "return to alcohol is a far more prevalent phenomenon than return to unlawful drugs. The reason is plain. Alcohol is legal. That is why there are twenty times as many alcoholics in the United States as there are heroin addicts."

The commission did not go on to point out, as it might have, that the difference in the way the Transit Authority treats rehabilitated drug addicts and alcoholics may reflect a certain cultural bias. The Transit Authority has always been dominated by Irish Catholics, a group which has had its share of alcoholics. Narcotics addiction is rarely found among Irish Catholics but is now a fairly common affliction of New York City blacks like Carl Beazer.

A typical response of employers to the New York State commission's inquiries came from a large carpet firm on Staten Island: "The reason for his dismissal was the fact that he was on a methadone program. . . . Mr. R. was a very willing worker . . . [but] we have a big plant and it is difficult to keep all areas and all personnel under observation at all times." A young woman discovered to be in a methadone program after urine testing of all employees, "was interviewed by the medical director and at that time admitted to being on a methadone program for two years. The doctor explained she had lied on the initial application and that was the reason for her termination. Miss Guiliano then asked the doctor if she had admitted to being on the methadone program would she have been hired. His answer was, 'probably no.' "

Bonding companies did not significantly discriminate against rehabilitated drug addicts. They made decisions on the basis of individual employees, without blanket rulings banning coverage to persons with histories of drug usage or even arrests and convictions connected with drug usage. "Discrimination which exists against rehabilitated addicts emanates from employers," said the commission, "who, only as a pretext, will categorically deny employment on the basis of an alleged inability to bond all rehabilitated addicts."

Outside of New York, drug addicts have an even tougher time getting jobs. Ironically, the great bias against addicts is an outgrowth of warnings against the dangers of drug addiction. Advertising campaigns in the mass media try to deter addiction by portraying all addicts as crazed and dysfunctional; campaigns, sometimes ordered by state legislatures, are carried on in the schools. The public image of a drug addict does not coincide with the image of a steady worker. An indication of employer attitudes is manifest in the response to efforts by the prestigious American Management Association in 1972 to schedule a series of seminars on how businesses could arrange for the treatment of addicted employees. Invitations to the seminars on "Drugs as a Management Problem" went out to fifty thousand businesses. Only four registrations came back.

The publications most popular among American businessmen

are filled with accounts of the danger to business if they hire drug addicts. Typical are articles like "Drug Abuse Is Your Headache Too," in the November 1970 issue of *Nation's Business;* "Workers' Use of Drugs Widespread in Nation," in the June 12, 1971, *New York Times;* and "The Rising Problem of Drugs on the Job," in the June 29, 1970, issue of *Time.* "The addict's sharply curtailed job performance," said the article in *Time,* "is only part of the problem for corporations—to support their habit, drug dependent workers often become pushers and ensnare co-workers into narcotic addiction."

The most lurid portrait of drug addicts I have encountered was offered some years ago by the New York City Police Department's journal, *Spring 3100:*

To be a confirmed drug addict is to be one of the walking dead. . . . The teeth have rotted out; the appetite is lost and stomach and intestines don't function properly. The gall bladder becomes inflamed; eyes and skin turn a bilious yellow. In some cases the membranes of the nose turn a flaming red; the partition separating the nostrils is eaten away—breathing is difficult. Oxygen in the blood decreases; bronchitis and TB develop. Sex organs become affected. Veins collapse and livid purplish scars remain. Nerves snap; vicious twitching develops. . . .

And so it went.

All this is in very marked contrast to the best contemporary studies of narcotics addicts. "Medical authorities now widely agree," Zinberg and Robertson say, "that even heroin and the opiates cause no physiological damage." [1] Even individuals who have regularly taken heroin of twenty and thirty times the purity and strength commonly available on American streets appear to function normally. Consumers Union said of thousands of Ameri-

1. Norman E. Zinberg and John A. Robertson, *Drugs and the Public* (New York: Simon and Schuster, 1972), p. 44.

can soldiers in Vietnam: "Despite daily use of doses of heroin far larger than those commonly available in the United States, these men continued to perform their military duties without detection, and in some cases with distinction. Indeed, military personnel addicted to heroin were indistinguishable to their superior officers from their unaddicted comrades-in-arms—so indistinguishable that military authorities found it necessary to introduce urine tests to identify heroin users." [2]

Physiological damage results from the manner in which street heroin is obtained and not from the effects of addiction. Bad living conditions, dirty needles, and adulterants do the damage, not the heroin. Dr. Andrew Weil has noted, "The problems associated with heroin (death from overdose; hepatitis; crime; mental and physical deterioration) appear to have no causal relationship to the pharmacological action of the drug. Rather they correlate better with features of the social context in which heroin exists in our country." [3]

Methadone maintenance programs do not end addiction. That is virtually impossible. Once a person is seriously attached to opiates, the chances are overwhelming that he will stay addicted. Methadone maintenance programs do transform the social context. The dangerous dirty needles and the adulterants are eliminated. The drugs are available legally and without cost. It is this transformation of the social context which enables a drug addict to live a normal life and hold down a steady job.

The medical literature has not yet succeeded in overcoming unfavorable public image. Fortunately, a thaw has begun in the home of the greatest number of addicts, New York City.

On March 22, 1972, the New York City Department of Personnel issued a policy statement that, except for the uniformed services, "A history of drug addiction shall not in itself constitute a

2. Edward Brecher, "Licit and Illicit Drugs," *The Consumers Union Report* (Boston: Little, Brown, 1972), p. 39.
3. A Report to the Ford Foundation, *Dealing with Drug Abuse* (New York: Praeger, 1972), p. 333.

bar to employment in any City position." [4] And, in September 1972, the Off-Track Betting Corporation in New York City announced it had been staffing one of its offices entirely with people in drug-treatment programs.

While it is still too early to offer more than very preliminary impressions, the criminal activity associated with drug addiction appears to be declining in New York and rising in the rest of the country. The decline started in New York well before the enactment of Nelson Rockefeller's draconian criminal penalties by the state legislature in 1973 and cannot be attributed to the fear of long prison sentences. It appears to reflect the relative availability of treatment programs and jobs for addicts. A recent court decision could improve matters in New York even further.

On March 21, 1974, the Appellate Division of New York State's Third Judicial Department decided the case of *Ahsaf v. Nyquist*. Carmen Ahsaf, a licensed practical nurse, started using heroin because she was then keeping company with an addict. Three months later she entered a hospital to get help but left after five days because, she claimed, there were more drugs in the hospital than in the street. She spent twenty-six days in another hospital for heroin detoxification and then checked into still another hospital for a month.

Carmen Ahsaf's next but unsuccessful try at kicking the habit was Phoenix House, a drug-free therapeutic community. In July 1970, she applied for acceptance in methadone programs. With long waiting lists, it took her nine months to get into a program. In the interim, she spent several months at Phoenix House and one of the state's commitment centers. Just before she started on methadone, she got a job at Flower Fifth Avenue Hospital. In December 1971, a petition was filed against her seeking revocation of her nursing license because she was a narcotics addict.

The Committee on Professional Conduct of the State Board of

4. It should be noted that the Department of Personnel has no jurisdiction over the New York City Transit Authority, which fired Carl Beazer.

Nursing recommended that Carmen Ahsaf's license be revoked but, because she was progressing well in the methadone maintenance program and had apparently not used heroin since enrolling in it, further recommended that the revocation be stayed and that she be placed on probation for five years. This did not satisfy the Board of Regents' Committee on Discipline, which decided to revoke Ms. Ahsaf's license unconditionally. The crucial factor for the Board of Regents was Carmen Ahsaf's "lack of candor" in two employment interviews. She had told the people at Flower Fifth Avenue Hospital that she was not using drugs.

"In this case, it seems to us that the Board of Regents has placed altogether too much emphasis on two instances of concealing relevant information from an employer," the Appellate Court said.

While we certainly do not condone lying, we can understand how a young, divorced, addicted mother might think it is justifiable to withhold relevant information in order to obtain employment which one expert testified was "the next most important factor," aside from the use of methadone and counseling, in the rehabilitation of a patient. There is nothing in this record to indicate that petitioner's [Ms. Ahsaf's] addiction affected the performance of her duties. To the contrary, her supervisors at the Flower Fifth Avenue Hospital testified that she was a competent nurse, that her performance evaluation contained ratings of "very good" or "satisfactory" in all categories, and that she had been given a merit raise in the course of her work. It is significant that despite petitioner's false statement to him in the interview and despite his knowledge of her enrollment in the methadone maintenance programs, Patrick Cussen, who hired her, stated that on the basis of her performance, he would continue to employ her.

All five judges on the Appellate Court concurred in reducing Carmen Ahsaf's penalty to the five years' probation recommended by the Committee on Professional Conduct of the State Board of Nursing.

Employment problems are not the only difficulties faced by people identified as drug users by record-keeping systems. During the 1960s, compulsory commitment programs were very popular. They were enacted to circumvent a 1961 Supreme Court decision that addiction *per se* was not a crime, and, therefore, addicts could not be put in prison just for being addicts. California adopted compulsory commitment in 1963 and New York in 1966. Old prisons were called hospitals, and guards were called counselors. But, seven years after he originally proposed the New York program, and after a billion dollars had been expended on it, Nelson Rockefeller conceded its failure. Nevertheless, the idea has not been entirely squelched.

In an interview reported in the *New York Times* (April 11, 1972) Dr. Jerome Jaffe, the psychiatrist who then headed President Nixon's Special Action Office for Drug Abuse Prevention (SAODAP) recommended that, "If one could just identify and take out of circulation the early users, we could break the whole chain [of drug use]." The *Times*'s story said, "Dr. Jaffe believes that with sufficient support from the media the public could be persuaded to support tests in schools and other institutions."

Jaffe's comments echo those of another Nixon adviser, Dr. Arnold Hutschneker. Both are attracted to the idea of taking out of circulation people who are troublesome—or in Hutschneker's case, people who are potentially troublesome. Jaffe's notions, like Hutschneker's, are being put into practice. The armed services regularly require urine tests to identify drug users. Urine tests have recently been adopted in several school systems. While touted as beneficial to those identified because treatment is offered, in practice they are punitive. Identification means discharge from the military or from school. The fantastically expensive failures of the compulsory commitment programs in

California and New York will slow up any effort to follow that path again. If the times should again make it expedient for a politician like Nelson Rockefeller to run for high office by campaigning against drug addicts, compulsory commitment could revive in popularity. The early identification testing for drug addiction, now growing in popularity in the schools and the armed services, would then have ominous consequences.

The federal government and the state governments have spent billions of dollars trying to cope with the problem. In any survey of popular attitudes, addiction emerges as one of the most pressing concerns. Only crime in the streets is a more immediate worry of residents of big cities, and it is closely related. Yet, the public desire to rehabilitate drug addicts is defeated at every turn by private fears.

6

The Crime of Illness
MENTAL HOSPITAL RECORDS

Myra Lee Glassman is a magna cum laude graduate of the City College of New York. In her junior year she made Phi Beta Kappa. She was an honors program student, won a New York State Regents Scholarship and a National Science Foundation grant for research in chemistry, and scored in the top one percent in science and quantitative ability on the national Medical College Admission test. Yet when she applied to thirteen medical schools she was turned down by all of them. The reason: Myra Lee Glassman was once a voluntary patient at Hillside Hospital in Queens, one of the country's outstanding psychiatric institutions.

With the help of the lawyer who headed the New York Civil Liberties Union's Mental Commitment project, Bruce Ennis, Ms. Glassman approached one of the medical schools and offered a plan to test her mental condition. She would submit to a current psychiatric examination and a review of her past history by any three psychiatrists of the college's choice. If any one of the three expressed the slightest doubt about her ability to succeed in medical school, she would not file suit. Nothing doing. She did file suit, relying in part on a section of the New York Mental Hygiene

Law which holds that "no person admitted to a hospital by voluntary or informal admission shall be deprived of any civil right solely by reason of such admission."

Although the right to attend an educational institution is a "civil right" in New York, the court ruled against her. The judge held she had been turned down not because she had once sought treatment in a mental hospital but because of the sickness which led her to seek treatment. As Ennis points out, this is like saying, "We are turning you down not because you are Negro, but because you have black skin and curly hair." [1]

While the trial was underway, Myra Lee Glassman applied to a fourteenth medical college and was accepted with a fellowship to participate in an unusual joint program in medicine and chemistry working toward degrees in both medicine and pharmacology. In 1974, she was in her fourth year and doing extremely well.

In the last few years, great public events have turned on public suspicions of people who have had psychiatric treatment. Senator Thomas Eagleton's history of treatment and failure to reveal it forced him to drop off the Democratic ticket as the party's candidate for vice president. Many people believe that the Eagleton episode, which raised the question of psychiatric treatment in an extraordinary context, started the McGovern campaign on the downhill skid.

White House "plumbers" broke into the office of Daniel Ellsberg's psychiatrist in search of information that could smear Ellsberg. Less well known is the earlier visit of FBI agents to the office of Ellsberg's wife's psychiatrist in New York to ask for damaging information about her. The psychiatrist refused to violate his patient's right to confidentiality, thereby possibly triggering the more circuitous effort to get her husband's file. Allegations that Richard Nixon and Gerald Ford had received psychiatric treatment from Dr. Arnold Hutschneker could, if proven, have been

---

1. Her case is described in greater detail in Bruce Ennis's book, *Prisoners of Psychiatry* (New York: Harcourt Brace Jovanovich, 1972).

extremely damaging. An unscrupulous opponent might have hired a burglar to search the files, but none did.

One person in ten spends some time in a mental hospital. Many more see psychiatrists. If information on psychiatric treatment were generally disseminated, it could cause incalculable harm. Information on private psychiatric treatment remains private usually. Psychiatrists are bound, as are all doctors, by the Hippocratic Oath, which reflects the historic respect for the confidentiality of a patient's relationship with a doctor. And, even the snoopiest of public and private agencies have neither the resources nor the ethics of the president who hired the "plumbers." There is less protection for patients in institutions. A private psychiatrist who knows his patients very well needs few records; institutional doctors, responsible for several hundred patients at a time, must rely on records of past diagnoses and staff observations. These records become a management device to maintain custody of patients with some efficiency. Kai Erikson and Daniel Gilbertson observe, "if a stranger were to notice how many of the hospital's resources were devoted to the task of recording information about patients, he might very well conclude that the main objective of the institution was to generate information and keep systematic files rather than to treat illness." [2]

While litigation was underway to challenge the conditions of confinement at Willowbrook, the giant New York State institution for the mentally retarded on Staten Island, attorney Bruce Ennis happened on a naked young woman alone in a locked room. He was told she was extremely violent, or so the attendants had been told. She had been in the cell longer than they had been employed; they had simply heard of her record. Ennis discovered that the twenty-three-year-old woman had been put in that room several years earlier, after she bit an attendant. He got her out of

2. In *On Record*, edited by Stanton Wheeler (New York: Russell Sage Foundation, 1969), p. 389.

the locked room; when he came back to Willowbrook, she was living about as normally as is possible in that institution. She invited him to her room and played a holiday season record for him.

The files mental hospitals keep, like those in most institutions with records, are generally limited to negative information. Case histories developed from a patient's encounter with a psychiatrist, write Erikson and Gilbertson, "supply a package of evidence to support the diagnosis made at admission." They make "it seem logical, reasonable, maybe even inevitable that the patient in question came to occupy the status in which he finds himself." [3]

Mental hospitals claim to deal with the "whole" person; therefore, they officially recognize no limits to what they consider relevant. In this, mental hospital records resemble school anecdotal records. The right of mental patients to know what is in those records has not been recognized. Progress has been made in establishing the right of students and their parents to see school records, and to limit their contents and insert in those records different versions of incidents; no comparable efforts have been made to circumscribe mental hospital records.

Despite the ancient rule that the confidentiality of a person's medical record is a privilege that belongs to the patient, not the doctor, mental hospital records tend to be seen as a convenience for the institution and, by law, as the property of the institution. Because the patient is, by definition, "crazy," any request he makes to see his own records is also considered crazy. In several states, this confidentiality is not recognized in law, however, and, while it rarely happens, psychiatrists and other doctors in those states can be forced to answer questions about communications with their patients. The laws in some states permit a patient to see his own records. Elsewhere, as in New York State, the records are

3. Ibid., p. 104.

available only after a lawsuit challenging illegal hospitalization has been filed on a patient's behalf. This procedure effectively discourages legal efforts to free patients from hospitals. Because it is impossible for a patient and his lawyer to see the records in advance to find out if a good case can be made out for releasing the patient, the guarded records serve to retain in mental hospitals patients who could otherwise be set free.

Restrictions on the right of patients to see their own records shield the institution from criticism. For a period of several years, Janet Gotkin was in and out of mental hospitals as a voluntary patient. Between 1962 and 1970 she spent periods at Hillside, Brooklyn State, and Gracie Square hospitals, all in New York. Now she is an organizer of Mental Patients Resistance of Westchester, one of a number of groups set up by ex–mental patients to protect their interests. Janet Gotkin, with her husband, set about to gather research for a book on institutional psychiatry. She tried to see her own records to check whether information on dates of admission, drug dosages, shock treatments, and test results was correct, and to compare the hospital's records of incidents with her own recollections. All three hospitals refused to let her look through her own records.

Police agencies seem able to get mental hospital records without much difficulty. Some states make these files available to all public agencies and even to insurance companies. The *contents* of these records are not readily accessible generally to other outsiders, yet the *fact* that a person has once been in a mental hospital becomes known fairly easily. If the expatient was confined for a long or even a brief period, there is a gap in his life that arouses the curiosity of a potential employer.

Henry Mercer, a man of many talents and eclectic interests, has boxed in Madison Square Garden, played semiprofessional baseball, delivered babies and saved victims of heart attacks as an ambulance attendant. In 1968, the New York City Hack License Bureau decided that Mercer was not qualified to drive a taxi. The reason: in 1949, when he was thirteen years old, he had been placed in a mental hospital.

Mercer was not crazy. His mother had died of a heart attack; his father was an alcoholic who beat him regularly; he had earned a couple of police Y.D. cards (see Chapter 4) for such offenses as hanging around pool halls and stealing an apple from a fruit stand; he cut school a lot because he was working at night, and when he was in school, he disrupted classes. The mental hospital was the only home authorities could find for him.

Rockland State Mental Hospital would have been willing to release Mercer at any time in the years that followed, but no one wanted him. He stayed in Rockland State for four years until he was seventeen, reading Plato and Emerson and living with the insane. Then an older brother got out of the Marine Corps and agreed to look after him.

Mercer worked for several years for Lincoln Hospital as a nurse's aid and ambulance attendant. He was graduated from night high school, married and had children, and became, in every way, a solid citizen. He had planned to drive a cab nights and weekends to earn extra money. When he was turned down, he collected statements from the director of Rockland State Hospital and five other psychiatrists that nothing about his mental condition should impair his ability to drive a cab. The Hack License Bureau persisted, despite the facts. It took several years and several court tests to win Mercer his license.[4]

Discrimination against former mental patients is growing worse. More people are expatients. Patients now stay in hospitals for shorter periods because psychiatrists increasingly recognize that confinement is anything but rehabilitative, because new medicines can long maintain many persons in normal job and home situations, and because the cost of extended confinement is

4. The story is told more fully in Ennis, *op. cit.*, p. 145.

becoming prohibitive. And, most important, civil liberties lawyers have made institutionalization even more expensive by "right to treatment" litigation. The court cases they bring have narrowed the legal grounds for holding people in hospitals and have won rights of periodic review for patients.

With shorter confinements and more available beds, hospitals admit more patients; the consequence is more and more ex-patients and more and more discrimination against them. The beachside town of Long Beach, Long Island, is a favorite refuge for ex–mental patients. Its many hotels and boardinghouses were originally built for summer vacationers. Now many are decayed, and inexpensive single rooms are available close to the beach. In late 1973, Long Beach passed an ordinance designed to make it impossible for expatients to live in that community.

The West Side of Manhattan is another community with old hotels which could serve as homes for discharged mental patients; yet, here too, despite the neighborhood's reputation for political liberalism, the prospect has aroused fears and antagonism.[5]

Laws barring housing to expatients, as Federal Judge Walter Bruchhausen made clear shortly after the Long Beach ordinance, cannot stand up against constitutional attack. The actions of Long Beach infringed upon "the right of citizens who are mentally ill to be treated in the least restrictive setting appropriate to their needs, and upon the right of such persons to choose their own places of residence, without unreasonable government interference." Landlords regularly discriminate against former patients without benefit of legal sanction. Employers discriminate against them even more often. Applications often inquire whether a person has ever been confined in a mental hospital. If the expatient lies, the employer may find out anyway.

5. Albert Blumenthal, who has represented the area in the state legislature for a decade, a spokesman for liberal causes, was quoted in the February 15, 1974, New York Times as saying, "There is an apparent effort to convert the hotels in this area into halfway houses for mental patients. I have expressed strong opposition to Dr. Miller [director of the New York State Department of Mental Hygiene]."

In many states, mental patients are fingerprinted, and their records are stored in criminal records data banks, as though they had been convicted of a crime. Some state laws authorize mental hospitals and the FBI to exchange information, and, in those states, the fingerprints are forwarded to the bureau. The records become available to employers from state data banks and the FBI just as arrest records do. The impact is comparable.

A specialized data bank for psychiatric records, known as the Multi-State Information System for Psychiatric Patients (MSIS), as of early 1974 stored records of patients from eight states and the District of Columbia. In January 1974, three patients, three doctors, and a psychiatric therapist at the Tremont Crisis Center in the Bronx filed suit against the Department of Mental Hygiene in New York, complaining that the department required that names, addresses, and Social Security numbers of patients go to the department for its central files. The information could be open to all persons and agencies participating in the Multi-State Information System.

The Tremont Crisis Center accepts patients only as outpatients; none live there. One patient who brought the suit said he would never have sought the psychiatric treatment he needs and wants at the Tremont Crisis Center had he known his name would appear in such centrally accessible records. The other two patients filing the suit would have at least "seriously reconsidered" the decision to get the help they need.

The relationship between doctor and patient, as between priest and penitent and lawyer and client, is held confidential in law precisely because it is regarded as good public policy for those in trouble to get help. The confidentiality of a relationship between psychiatrist and patient, closely guarded in private care, is not protected when a patient needs institutional care. Then, the bureaucratic tendency to gather and record information gains the upper hand over privacy. The institution takes priority over the individual. The lesson is: avoid institutional care. Unfortunately, most who need psychiatric help cannot afford private care. Their choice is either to go without needed care or risk stigmatization.

Nonpsychiatric medical hospitals, legal services agencies, and organized churches, also involved in confidential relationships, have not made comparable demands for information. Psychiatric institutions, on the other hand, apparently do not regard service to patients as their exclusive or even primary concern. At least as important in their view, as Erving Goffman has noted, is their role in protecting "the community from the danger and nuisance of certain kinds of misconduct. . . ." [6]

Understood in that way, a psychiatric institution is more like a prison punishing a criminal than a hospital serving a patient. It should not be surprising that the tradition represented by the Hippocratic Oath, which is as important to a private psychiatrist as to any medical doctor, is held in such low regard by many psychiatric institutions. The institution is in business to serve other interests than those of its patients.

6. *Asylums* (Garden City, New York: Anchor Books, 1961) p. 352.

7

Inaptitude, Apathy, and Bed-wetting
DISCHARGE RECORDS

Walter Rose got out of the air force in 1961 with an honorable discharge. Like many other veterans, he found his discharge papers an asset in getting a job. He didn't know that the papers told employers more than they told him. The people who hired him understood a code number, SDN514, on the discharge papers which had been kept secret from Rose.

Several years later, Rose (not his real name) decided to change jobs. Honorable discharge papers in hand, he went for interviews. This time he got some funny looks. The code number on his discharge papers, SDN514, had meant a hardship discharge back in 1961. Now the air force had given it a new meaning; now it had been changed to mean homosexual.

SDN is the air force's acronym for Separation Designation Number. The army and navy equivalent is SPN, which stands for Separation Program Number. Every veteran discharged between 1955 and March 1974 has an SPN or SDN number on his discharge papers. Most of the 530 numbers used (see Appendix) were free of stigma. But in 1973 alone, 35,640 men who got out with honorable or general (under honorable conditions) discharges had "unsuitable" SPN numbers; 21,000 were coded as "character or behavior disorders"; another 10,000 were branded: "defective attitudes, and an inability to expend effort constructively." Other secret codes said a veteran had "homosexual tendencies" or was a "shirker" or was guilty of "disloyalty or subversion" or "unacceptable conduct."

In all, about a million veterans have been given derogatory discharge codes. And, although the veterans themselves did not know the meaning of the codes, the personnel departments of Firestone, Boeing, Chrysler, Standard Oil of California, and many other major employers did. They knew what to look for on a veteran's discharge papers.

Before the meaning of some of these codes was first publicized in March 1973, victimized veterans had no idea what they meant. Publicity did not reach everyone affected. Many honorably discharged veterans with stigmatizing numbers are probably still mystified by the difficulties they have faced in getting jobs.[1]

But the problem was not simply the secrecy of the codes but the labels themselves.

David Addlestone, the lawyer who directs the ACLU's Military Rights Project, secured the first court order against SPN codes in February 1974. In a case challenging the army's program for discovering soldiers in the European Command who used drugs, Federal District Judge Gerhard Gesell said that the drug searches could go forward, "so long as evidence or information obtained as a result of such procedures is not used as a basis for any punitive action, including judicial and nonjudicial punishment under the Uniform Code of Military Justice and administrative discharge other than honorable discharge unaccompanied by any indication—by SPN code or otherwise—of drug use, unfitness or unsuitability."

Six weeks after Gesell's ruling the Defense Department announced it was abandoning SPN and SDN numbers. Veterans with unfavorable code numbers could now obtain new discharge

1. The list of the codes and their translation is reproduced in the Appendix to this book, see page 201.

papers free of such numbers. However, the Pentagon refused to go along with the demands of the ACLU and several other groups that it recall for repair defective discharge papers just as General Motors recalls defective cars. Lieutenant General Leo E. Benade has responded for the Pentagon saying, "There is no practical method of individually notifying the 18 million veterans who have been discharged since the early 1950s." The response ignores one fact: it would only be necessary to notify the one million or so veterans with unfavorable codes. Not only does the Department of Defense have records showing which veterans have such codes, but, since the beginning of 1965, the army's records and, by the end of 1968, the records of all the other services had been computerized. A simple mailing to the addresses on file with the Defense Department or the Veterans Administration would reach a very large number of men. Such a mailing would spread the word so that many other veterans could ask that the stigmatizing SPN numbers be erased from their discharge papers. The Department of Defense took no such steps to ensure that "honorable" discharge papers were free from codes like SPN 388, "Unfitness—sexual perversion"; SPN 28F, "Unfitness—an established pattern for showing dishonorable failure to pay just debts"; and SPN 440, "Separation for concealment of serious arrest record." Evidence is emerging that the code labels have sometimes been parting gifts from vindictive officers or simply clerical errors.

By the summer of 1974, it appeared that the Defense Department was reneging on its announced intention to stop pinning derogatory labels on servicemen getting out with honorable discharges. According to General Benade, the services will start keeping narrative descriptions of the reasons for discharges. This narrative will be available to the veteran on his request. This is being done purportedly to give "some additional element of privacy to individuals who might not wish to release their reason for discharge." The trouble with this new system is that any potential employer may now insist that a veteran furnish a copy of the narrative statement as a condition for employment. Combined with the Defense Department's refusal to seek out the victims of almost twenty years of secret codes, the new plans largely vitiate what appeared a significant victory against dossier-mongers just a few months earlier.

In addition to the veterans haunted by derogatory codes on their honorable discharge papers, about another million who got less than honorable discharges during the last twenty years have been harassed. Among them was William L. Harvey, a twenty-year-old black marine, convicted by a general court-martial at Camp Pendleton, California. His crime: making disloyal statements with intent to promote disloyalty among the troops in violation of Article 134 of the Uniform Code of Military Justice. He was convicted for these statements to fellow marines:

Specification 1

(1) Why should the black man go to Vietnam and fight the white man's war and then come back and have to fight the white man?

(2) That he (Lance Corporal Harvey) was not going to fight in Vietnam and neither should Private Jones.

Specification 2

(1) Why should you (Private Johnson) go to Vietnam? Your people are over here fighting, why should you go over there and fight when you have to fight a war over here?

Specification 3

(1) The black man should not go to Vietnam and fight the white man's war.

(2) That PFC James Charles Griffin should not go to Vietnam to fight the white man's war.

(3) That PFC James Charles Griffin was an "Uncle Tom" for wanting to go to Vietnam to fight the white man's war.

Specification 4

(1) You should request Mast with the Captain (Company Commander) and refuse to go to Vietnam because there is no reason for you and the rest of the black men to go over to Vietnam and fight the white man's war.

(2) You should request Mast before the Company Commander and refuse to go fight the war in Vietnam.

According to testimony at Harvey's trial, he said these things during a five- to ten-minute period on July 27, 1967, while the members of his unit, mostly black, were eating noon chow in the field under a tree, listening to a portable record player, and discussing a newspaper story on the ghetto riots then erupting in Detroit.

Harvey was sentenced to six years in prison and a dishonorable discharge. He was lucky. Another black marine accused in the same incident, PFC George Daniels, got a ten-year sentence. After they had served about two years in prison, the Court of Military Appeals found that Harvey had not made disloyal statements and reversed that part of the conviction. It held that the lesser offense of solicitation to disobey orders had been established. The prison sentence was reduced to four months, twenty months less than the time Harvey had already served. He was paid $1,400 for loss of pay during the time he was wrongfully imprisoned. His discharge was changed from dishonorable to undesirable.

After Harvey's discharge, two United States Courts of Appeals found Article 134 under which he had been tried unconstitutional. However, those decisions were reversed by the United States Supreme Court on June 19, 1974. In a six-to-three decision, Article 134 was upheld.

The new, undesirable, discharge did not free Harvey. He has been denied most veterans' benefits. He could not go to school under the G.I. Bill. He did get accepted in professional training programs, first at the John Hancock Insurance Company and then with the New York Telephone Company, only to be turned away when he revealed his undesirable discharge.

In 1973, after four years out of the military prison without a steady job, Harvey took a desperate step. He went to the Mayor's Office for Veterans Action in New York City and asked for help in getting a job. He said he had received a general discharge, one notch higher than he actually received. The Mayor's Office for Veterans Action got him a job, not in a professional training program, but as a nurse's aide at the United States Public Service Hospital on Staten Island. When he reported for work he was asked to produce his military discharge papers. He did so, only to be told he was fired. This time, his offense was lying. William Harvey is a hard man to keep down. When last heard from he had opened his own karate school.

Veterans who get dishonorable or bad conduct discharges are even worse off than Harvey. They are denied all Veterans Administration benefits, including compensation for service-connected disability or death, vocational rehabilitation, hospitalization, domiciliary care, medical and dental care. They are refused federal civil service preference, federal civil service retirement, job counseling, and employment placement. A veteran crippled in Vietnam, who may require intensive medical treatment for the rest of his life, could get no care at a VA hospital if he was once found guilty of disobeying an officer and had received a dishonorable discharge.

For veterans like Harvey who have undesirable discharges the Veterans Administration has the power to decide whether to give benefits. In 95 percent of all cases, however, the Veterans Administration decides to withhold benefits from such veterans.

One veteran not included among the 5 percent of the undesirably discharged on whom the VA takes pity is Thomas Aiken, Jr. His eye was injured in March 1968 in a fragmentation bomb explosion on the road to Quang Tri in Vietnam. Aiken won combat medals in Vietnam, yet received an undesirable discharge for going home for Christmas a day early while stationed at Fort Knox, Kentucky. The Veterans Administration chose to deny his request for medical attention. In 1972, his eye was removed. It might have been saved if Aiken had received prompt medical attention. Now, Aiken's chances of getting a job are limited by the lack of an eye as well as by his discharge. He wears a patch since he cannot afford to buy a glass eye because he can't get a steady job.

A soldier can get an undesirable discharge for a number of reasons. If a soldier is charged with an offense, whether guilty or not, he can resign rather than face court-martial. This resembles plea bargaining in the civilian courts. He will take an undesirable discharge rather than risk being convicted. At the time, it seems the easy way out. If convicted, he may serve time in a military prison *and* get a bad discharge. Few soldiers in such circumstances are aware of the lifelong consequences of the bad discharge that goes with resignation. The gamble that he *might* be acquitted in a court-martial doesn't appear worthwhile, even to an innocent man.

A soldier can also be undesirably discharged for unfitness, misconduct, or security reasons. A serviceman threatened with an undesirable discharge has the right to a hearing before an administrative discharge board. If he exercises this right, the hearing takes place before a board of three officers, none of whom need have any legal training. The board is not bound by rules of evidence, cannot compel witnesses, and may receive testimony kept secret from the serviceman. It does not require the government to bear the burden of proof. Its findings and recommendations need not even be disclosed to the serviceman. Factual errors made by the board will be hard to run down.

To the employers who hired and then fired William Harvey, the distinction between an undesirable discharge and a dishonorable discharge probably wasn't very meaningful. In fact, when it comes to getting a job, anything less than an honorable discharge, even a general discharge, is likely to be a serious handicap.

An air force manual says that a general discharge is a "definite disadvantage to [a veteran] seeking civilian employment." The army says that a veteran with a general discharge "may expect to encounter substantial prejudice in civilian life." A federal court in California found that a general discharge is "a stigma of tremendous impact." Nevertheless, a serviceman has no right to a hearing to challenge a general discharge unless he has eight or more years of continuous active military service. And even eight-year veterans have a right to a hearing to challenge only certain kinds of general discharges.

The Vietnam war produced more than 400,000 less than honorable discharges. In the years 1965–1973, there were 229,792 general discharges, 162,919 undesirable, 27,292 bad conduct, and 2,865 dishonorable. Most of these discharges are not based on criminal activity but on such vague criteria as "character or behavior disorders." According to a Department of Defense study, 72 percent of all general discharges were for this class of offenses. Less than honorable discharges could be given for such offenses as "shirking," "inaptitude," "apathy," "enuresis (bed-wetting)," "alcoholism," "drug addiction," "homosexual and other aberrant tendencies," "unsanitary habits," and "financial irresponsibility."

In 1971, "inaptitude" accounted for 8,247 less than honorable discharges, "character and behavior disorders" (the largest category) accounted for 27,806, "apathy" 6,749, and 319 poor souls were given bad discharges for "enuresis (bed-wetting)."

The Department of Defense's explanations of what the vague categories on this list mean do not do a great deal to clarify matters. A Pentagon directive defines "inaptitude" as: "Applicable to those persons who are best described as inapt due to lack of general adaptability, want of readiness of skill, unhandiness, or inability to learn." "Apathy" is defined as: "a significant observable defect, apparently beyond the control of the individual, elsewhere not readily describable."

Such discharges are usually based on decisions by commanding officers. Not surprisingly, they are disproportionately the lot of minority group members who received them two and a half times as often as their numbers in the service would seem to warrant.

The disparity between blacks and whites reflects the impact of records acquired before they entered the service. Many of the blacks were school dropouts or push-outs. They were assigned to outfits concerned with food service, supply, and transportation rather than those which required greater technical skills. A 1972 Department of Defense Task Force report noted that this contributed to the "greater proportion of job dissatisfaction complaints on the part of black personnel, which in turn, may have a bearing on the disciplinary action rate of this minority group."

The racial impact of bad discharges could get worse. During the Vietnam era, blacks made up about 11 percent of the armed forces. However, after the end of the draft in 1973, the proportion of black enlistments began to rise. For two months in the summer of 1973, blacks accounted for 30 percent of the enlistments in the army. While black enlistments may not remain at this level in the army and are unlikely to reach this level in other services, the overall percentage of blacks in the armed forces will probably rise, perhaps to the 20 percent level. They go into the armed forces to take advantage of the rising pay rates and because they cannot get jobs elsewhere. However, if they leave the armed forces with bad discharges, their chances of getting civilian jobs will be a lot worse than if they had never enlisted.

Among the Veterans Administration programs from which many less-than-honorably discharged veterans are excluded are those supposed to treat drug addicts. It is a vicious cycle. Honorable discharges are not available to drug addicts. The Veterans Administration drug treatment programs are only available to those veterans who don't need them. Most of the 60,000 or so Vietnam-era veterans (VA estimate) who emerged from the armed forces addicted to heroin have the alternative of contemplating the wonders of Catch 22.

The Emergency Employment Act of 1971 provides financial assistance to local governments for public service employment. It specifies that preference is to be given to veterans "who served in the Armed Forces in Indo-China or Korea or after August 5, 1954."

Tommy Thompson was employed, at the end of 1971, as an operator helper at the Plaquemine, Louisiana, city diesel plant. His job was to keep the plant clean and ready for power production in case of a breakdown at the steam plant. Six weeks later, Plaquemine passed this ordinance: "Resolved that any person employed by the City of Plaquemine or by the Emergency Employment Act, if said person is a veteran, must have an Honorable Discharge and must be a man of good character." The next day Tommy Thompson was fired because he had an undesirable discharge.

Thompson filed suit. His ACLU lawyer charged, among other things, that the exclusion of all veterans not honorably discharged was a bill of attainder and an ex post facto law. The lawsuit described the Plaquemine ordinance as "a clumsy instrument." As it turned out Thompson got his job back because the city of Plaquemine was so clumsy.[2]

The U.S. Court of Appeals for the Fifth Circuit, in December 1973, found no rational relationship between Thompson's discharge and the city's interest in maintaining the quality of its work

2. Plaquemine's national reputation does not rest on subtlety. The community's best known public figure was the late Leander Perez, a lawyer, millionaire, and political boss of Plaquemine, best known as one of the South's most vituperative and intractable racists. Perez once provoked Governor Earl Long of Louisiana to scold him for his defiance of the federal government and to demand: "What are you gonna do now, Leander, now that the feds have got the A-bomb?"

force. The decision will be a helpful precedent in other court cases.

In most other communities, a less than honorable discharge would have been held against Thompson without a law or written policy absolutely prohibiting his employment. An unwritten policy would have been a poorer target for litigation than the Plaquemine law. And, because that is the way these things usually work, there is no court case other than Tommy Thompson's holding that veterans without honorable discharges are entitled to jobs.

The decision in Tommy Thompson's case may have its greatest immediate impact on hiring for police and fire departments. They often have announced policies giving preference to veterans in employment and requiring honorable discharges. The federal Equal Employment Opportunities Commission recently found a fire department's exclusion of veterans without honorable discharges (and its bias against men with arrest records) racially discriminatory. Only 9.8 percent of the fire department's work force was black, while 41 percent of the city's population and 20 percent of the metropolitan area was black.

More than 300,000 Vietnam-period veterans live in New York City. Deputy Mayor Edward Morrison testified at hearings of the City Commission on Human Rights in March 1973, that about 15 percent or about 45,000 of them were unemployed. The national unemployment rate was about 5½ percent and the unemployment rate for veterans, according to the VA, about 8 percent. The Veterans Administration figures did not include the veterans with bad discharges; it seems to regard them as nonpersons. Morrison had included veterans without honorable discharges in his 15 percent.

"I have an undesirable discharge because I had joined the American Servicemen's Union," said one veteran with a bad discharge who testified at the same hearings as Morrison. "I have not been able to find a job. I am ineligible for veteran's welfare—that

$17 a week plus rent that the brothers have to wait four to five hours in the morning for and have to go through all kinds of harassment for and have to discuss the most intimate matters of their personal life with these dudes to get. So I have to commit crimes of survival. And I am going to lead my brothers wherever we have to go to get jobs and decent benefits."

Not only jobs are denied to those who don't have the right papers from the armed forces. As another veteran testified at the New York City hearings: "Middle income housing is available for veterans but it is through the VA and, if you have a less than honorable discharge, don't bother going to the VA, they won't talk to you."

Another veteran who testified at the commission hearings told about still another problem facing veterans, the reenlistment code:

MR. DANIELS: "The government told me I had a skill as an expert aircraft mechanic. But industry doesn't want me. The whole deal was just a big nightmare. I'm sorry I ever came back. . . . Whether or not I had any practical experience did not mean anything to [industry]. The one thing they wanted to see was DD form 214 discharge, which contains a reenlistment code—whether the service would like you to reenlist. My code happens to be a Code 2. It means that you cannot go back in the service. Somehow big business and the government work hand-in-hand, so they consider anybody with anything higher than Code 1 [reenlistment recommended] bad news."

COMMISSIONER NORTON: "Was yours an honorable discharge?"

MR. DANIELS: "Yes. The New York Times had an ad for an aircraft refueling supervisor. I was a sergeant in the air force. I crewed Phantom aircraft, recon and bombers. I had almost four years of training and three years of practical experience. I was assistant line supervisor in Vietnam. I brought all my records down to this man—'Did you ever have any prior civilian experience?' he asked. I said, 'I worked under war conditions. I have been shot at and mortar attacked and I have been a supervisor. You name it and I have done it.' But, he said I wasn't qualified enough to work on a civilian aircraft . . .

And the Welfare said I am not eligible for welfare, I am eligible to work. So there might be some heads that have to be cracked open."

Another veteran testified:

I got my 214 [discharge papers] in the mail. They said, "We don't need you; your body is torn and twisted, your legs are shot; we don't want you any more." I was in no way derogatory towards the service. They just said "banned from reenlistment"—because of my disability.

Several efforts at legal reform are underway. Senator Sam Ervin of North Carolina, a longtime critic of military discharges, has sponsored legislation which would require due process of law before less than honorable discharges could be given. Ervin notes that under the present procedures, the serviceman facing a bad discharge "has no right to confront the witnesses against him. He has no right to compel the production of evidence. There is no requirement that any competent evidence be in the record to support the finding. In short, the proceedings are almost completely lacking in what we in Anglo-American jurisprudence think of as fundamental due process."

A more radical legislative proposal, thus far supported by a mere handful in the House of Representatives, would wipe out all categories of discharges and prohibit the disclosure of any information on why a man or woman was discharged to anyone outside the armed forces. Such sweeping reform is unlikely any time soon.

Representative John Seiberling of Ohio, a member of the Judiciary Committee seen by television viewers in the impeachment proceedings, has taken a special interest in the problem of bad discharges and SPN numbers. He sent a questionnaire to the nation's hundred largest corporations asking for their employment policies affecting veterans. Seventy-four corporations responded and admitted the following kinds of discrimination: 41 percent said they discriminated against veterans with general discharges, 61 percent against veterans with undesirable discharges, 62 percent against veterans with bad conduct discharges, and 73 percent against veterans with dishonorable discharges.

"The figures I cite represent only the admitted discrimination," said Seiberling in a statement on the floor of Congress on November 28, 1973. "The percentage of corporations which actually discriminate may be substantially higher." He notes that 80 percent of the corporations responding said they require veterans applying for jobs to submit a copy of their DD-214 discharge certificates. This certificate would reveal an unfavorable discharge and the SPN number. Twenty percent of the responding corporations admitted they could decode the SPN numbers. Seiberling was convinced that remedial legislation was necessary to "help make employable many thousands of veterans who have been unfairly denied access to jobs because of the unwise discharge policies of the Defense Department."

Lawyers like David Addlestone of the ACLU are pressing the Department of Defense to establish offices around the country to which veterans could apply to upgrade their discharges. Now the services discharge review boards are in Washington, D.C.; most veterans with bad discharges find it difficult and prohibitively expensive to travel there to appear before such a board. Without a personal appearance the chances of upgrading a discharge are poor. The relative inaccessibility of the military review boards denies many veterans the opportunity to go to court to upgrade their discharges because courts insist that veterans first exhaust their administrative remedies. And that means going to Washington.

A decentralized procedure for "upgrading" discharges may be set up by President Ford's Clemency Board. It is unlikely to be of much help to veterans with bad discharges. The "clemency discharge" it can grant may prove a larger stigma than any other bad discharge.

The Vietnam war killed 55,000 Americans, wounded another 300,000, and left behind over 400,000 veterans with bad discharges and a similar number with bad discharge codes. Richard Nixon's public adulation of the POWs notwithstanding, the Vietnam veterans did not return like the conquering heroes who came back from earlier wars. Not for them were the fireboats, dancing girls, parades, and parties which bring back nostalgic memories to World War II veterans. The public dislike of the Vietnam war has rubbed off on its veterans.

To be a veteran of World War II was to have an advantage in getting a job, not so with Vietnam veterans. Some employers distrust them as hawks who are to blame for the war. Other employers worry about whether they became addicted to drugs while in the service.

Of 518 men held for trial in the Essex County Jail in Newark in September 1973, because of inability to afford bail, 35 percent were Vietnam-era veterans.

The war was a loser, and its veterans are seen as losers. The biggest losers of them all are those stigmatized in the dossiers by bad discharges or honorable discharges with bad codes.

8

Not a Suitable Person

ARREST RECORDS

On January 18, 1970, Paul Cowan was arrested in Brooklyn for possession of marijuana. Two months later the charge was dismissed. In September 1970, he moved to Boston and applied for a license to drive a cab. A hack license was issued, but a week later he was ordered to report to the Boston Police Department's Bureau of General Services. His license was being revoked. The reason: a routine check with the Federal Bureau of Investigation had disclosed an "open" charge of possession of narcotics pending in New York.[1] His protest that the charge had been dismissed did no good. On March 12, 1971, Paul Cowan received formal notice that his license had been revoked because he was "not a suitable person to be so licensed."

Cowan's story is unusual in only one respect. He found out why he lost his job. Most people who are denied jobs because of arrest records never learn why.

In 1967, the President's Commission on Law Enforcement issued a series of comprehensive reports on crime in America that are still considered the definitive findings on the subject. The

---

1. It is customary for law enforcement agencies to escalate charges involving marijuana into "narcotics arrests" when reporting them to employers. Since there are now more than 400,000 marijuana arrests nationwide annually, the devastating impact can be readily imagined.

commission found that 58 percent of white urban males, like Paul Cowan, will be arrested at some time during their lives. The figure for black urban males is 90 percent. For U.S. males in all categories, 50 percent will be arrested; for all females, 12 percent. Like Paul Cowan, many arrested are not convicted. Of about 8.6 million persons arrested each year for all criminal acts other than traffic offenses, about 4 million are not convicted. They are presumed innocent. In practice, they often suffer consequences as grave as if they had been guilty.

The FBI is the primary source of arrest-record information. As a matter of routine, almost all police departments in the country forward to the bureau for filing the fingerprints of persons they have arrested. (All persons fingerprinted upon induction into the armed services are also on record in the FBI fingerprint files.) Testifying in the case of *Menard v. Mitchell* in 1970 (the name of the case at that time—it started as *Menard v. Clark* and now goes under the name of *Menard v. Saxbe)*, a bureau official reported that, on an average working day, the FBI's Identification Division got 29,000 sets of fingerprints in the mail. Only 13,000 came from law-enforcement agencies. The remaining 16,000 sets were sent in by banks, insurance companies, government employers (municipal, county, state, and federal), licensing agencies, and the like. In return, these agencies received from the FBI any information it had in its files on the 29,000 persons whose prints came in that day. That's how Paul Cowan's Brooklyn arrest record got to the people who give out hack licenses in Boston.

The bureau has been efficient about gathering and disseminating arrest records; it has been rather careless about including data on what happens to the people *after* arrest. In the Menard case, the special agent in charge of the FBI's Identification Division, Beverly Ponder, grew a little testy when questioned about this by a volunteer lawyer for the National Capital Area Civil Liberties Union, Raymond Twohig:

TWOHIG: Does the FBI make any effort to obtain final dispositions where requests are received for arrest records? Before disseminating those arrest records?

PONDER: We urge the contributors [to the FBI fingerprint files] to submit to us final dispositions, but we don't go out and try to pick them up.

Ponder testified that there is no statistic available within the FBI on the final dispositions that have been recorded in the bureau's files; he knew of no way to make an intelligent estimate. That helps to explain why the Boston hack-licensing people weren't told the charges against Paul Cowan had been dismissed.

On July 1, 1974, a new FBI policy went into effect. The bureau continues to disseminate arrest records to law enforcement agencies whether or not it has any information on what happened after arrest. However, now arrest records given to banks and state and local agencies for employment and licensing purposes must be accompanied by a report of the disposition of the arrest unless it is less than one year old. The exception for arrests less than a year old is to allow time for court action after the arrest. The new policy set up by FBI Director Clarence Kelley does not allow for the possibility that law enforcement agencies getting dossiers from the bureau without any information on disposition will, in turn, forward that information to employers.

Some employers are not interested in arrests, only convictions. One such, it was thought, was the Federal Civil Service Commission.

TWOHIG: Is the FBI aware that recently Federal job-application forms were changed, and the question which asked if the applicant was arrested now asks if he has been convicted?

PONDER: Yes, I am aware of that.

TWOHIG: Do Federal agencies, in particular civil-service commissions, receive at present all information about arrests—or only arrests with convictions—when they apply to the FBI?

PONDER: They receive all the material that appears on the identification records.

TWOHIG: And that includes conviction and nonconviction arrests?

PONDER: That is correct.

The circumstances of this case were these: Dale Menard, a former marine, had been arrested and detained for two days by the Los Angeles police for "suspicion of burglary." He was never convicted or even charged with a crime. In fact, it is not clear a crime had been committed by anyone. Menard had the misfortune to be sitting on a park bench when the police received a telephone complaint about a prowler in the neighborhood. With the help of the National Capital ACLU, Menard sued to remove his arrest record from the files of the FBI and to stop the FBI from reporting his record to potential employers. Menard's suit has been in court for six years. It was heard twice by the United States Court of Appeals in the District of Columbia. On April 23, 1974, that court decided that Menard could compel the FBI to expunge his record because "the FBI is statutorily precluded from maintaining in its criminal files as an arrest record an encounter with the police that has been established not to constitute an arrest." By treating the detention and failure to charge Menard as less than arrest, the Court of Appeals postponed to another day a broad ruling on whether the FBI could maintain and disseminate records of arrests not leading to convictions.

Two months after the Court of Appeals decision, Dale Menard's attorneys were informed that the fingerprints had been expunged from the FBI files and returned to the Los Angeles police. The bureau also said it had passed on this intelligence to the Department of Defense's National Agency Check Center, Fort Holabird, Maryland, and the United States Marine Corps since it had previously sent his prints there. If Menard and his attorneys wanted to destroy all copies of the fingerprints taken at the time of his arrest, six years after first filing suit against the FBI, they would have to take on the Department of Defense, the marine corps and the Los Angeles police!

Back in June 1971, the Menard case was the subject of a controversial decision by Federal District Judge Gerhard Gesell. He ordered the FBI to stop giving out arrest records to anyone but law-enforcement agencies, and then only for law-enforcement purposes. Gesell found "that Congress never intended to or did in fact authorize dissemination of arrest records to any state or local agency for purposes of employment or licensing checks." He concluded that the arrest-record distribution system "is out of effective control."

Congress acted quickly to overturn the order. It passed a bill, introduced by Senators Alan Bible and Howard Cannon of Nevada, to make FBI arrest data available to "any non–law-enforcement official or agency" authorized to get the information by state or local law. The two senators said they were particularly concerned to make sure data was available to Nevada's gaming industry so people with arrest records would be kept out.

The case for the bureau's role of maintaining and disseminating arrest records was set forth by L. Patrick Gray III, then acting director of the FBI, in a written response to a question from Maryland's Senator Charles Mathias, Jr., of the Senate Judiciary Committee, then considering Gray's nomination as permanent director of the FBI. "The arrest-record files of the FBI Identification Division as well as those of many state and local identification bureaus are replete with lengthy arrest records of longtime hoodlums and members of organized crime whose arrests never resulted in conviction," said Gray. "Many sex offenders of children are not prosecuted because parents of the victim do not want to subject the child to the traumatic experience of testifying. Others are not tried because key evidence has been suppressed or witnesses are, or have been, made unavailable. The latter situation is not uncommon in organized-crime cases. To prohibit dissemination of such arrest records would be a disservice to the public upon whom they [persons with records] might prey again."

Gray speculated about "the potential school teacher with two prior rape arrests and no convictions" and "a police applicant with a prior Peeping Tom arrest and no conviction." Given these possibilities, "the rationale for disseminating arrest records not supported by convictions is substantial," said Gray.

Gray's view, of course, equates arrests with convictions. It turns upside down the presumption of innocence and provides for punishment by means of record dissemination for persons the courts could not or would not convict.

Many live in fear because of old arrest records. One such person is Jane Morris (not her real name). In 1947, at the age of 20, she married a man of whom her parents disapproved. She moved to California and lived under a different name. When her husband was arrested there and charged with transporting stolen property across state lines, Jane Morris was arrested as an accessory. They were returned to Michigan where they were rearrested on the same charges. He was convicted and the charges against her dismissed.

In the process, Jane Morris learned some things about her husband which led her to secure an annulment of her marriage and full custody of her infant son. She set out to rebuild her life, remarried, earned a Ph.D. and an educational doctorate, published many articles in professional journals, and became a high-ranking official in a large urban school system. Though she has received important awards for accomplishments in her profession, she is haunted by fear of disclosure of her early life. The FBI records her arrests in California and again when she was returned to Michigan, but shows no disposition. She has written to the ACLU:

I am left with the burden of providing proof that my case has been disposed of.

WORSE—I am forced to reveal the unpleasant details and relive the traumatic experience all over again. AND WORST OF ALL—I am at the mercy of any employer, actual or potential, who, in essence, has been granted the right by the FBI to examine these facts and to serve as judge and jury all over again.

Jane Morris's letter to the ACLU was prompted by the adoption of a new system in her city for checking on the past records of school officials. Her record has "prevented me from applying for many other positions. At this very moment, this information still serves to threaten my professional life."

Opposition to the dissemination of arrest records is mounting. Illinois has passed a law making it an unfair labor practice to deny a job because of an arrest. A similar measure was adopted by the New York State Legislature in early 1974 but vetoed by Governor Malcolm Wilson. About the same time, Governor Thomas Meskill of Connecticut also vetoed such legislation, but his veto was overriden by a resounding vote of both houses of the state's legislature. Significant movement toward comprehensive arrest records legislation is under way in the Congress.

For the past few years, Representative Don Edwards of California and Senators Quentin Burdick of North Dakota and Sam Ervin of North Carolina have sponsored measures to control the dissemination of arrest records. Hearings were held in 1972 and again in 1973. The bills had little support.

By 1974, the support for such legislation had grown dramatically. The Watergate revelations made privacy a front-page issue. Richard Nixon, whose administration had become synonymous with governmental intrusion on privacy, felt obliged to discuss the question in his State of the Union Message. And on February 23, 1974, Nixon addressed the nation on "The American Right of Privacy."

While the Nixon address was as notable for what it left out [2] as for what it left in, it was the first presidential pronouncement on arrest records. "In some instances the information itself is inaccurate and has resulted in the withholding of credit or jobs from deserving individuals," said Nixon. "In other cases, obsolete information has been used, such as arrest records which have not been updated to show that the charges made against an individual were subsequently dropped or the person found innocent. In many cases, the citizen is not even aware of what information is held on record, and if he wants to find out, he either has nowhere to turn or else he does not know where to turn." Nixon went on to note that, "Earlier this month, Attorney General Saxbe proposed legislation to the Congress which would establish rules governing the collection and use of criminal justice information."

The bill to which Nixon referred was S.2964, introduced on February 5, 1974, by Senator Hruska and cosponsored by Senators Ervin, Brooke, Byrd, Burdick, Fong, Gurney, Mathias, Roth, Scott, Thurmond, and Young. The same group of senators, not including Gurney but joined by Kennedy, Tunney, and Mansfield, joined in introducing S.2963, of which Senator Ervin was the principal sponsor. While S.2963 placed far greater limitations on the dissemination of arrest records than S.2964, adoption of either bill would drastically limit their availability.[3]

Articles on the subject (including an earlier version of this chapter in the *New York Times Magazine*) appeared in several magazines and newspapers. Several had discussed the development of the FBI's computerized National Crime Information Center. In operation since 1967, NCIC had been placed under FBI control in 1970. By the end of 1973 it housed some 4.8 million records on wanted criminals and on stolen cars, firearms, securities, and other stolen property and was linked by computer with

---

2. The address contained no mention of political surveillance, a topic that also went unmentioned in a detailed 5,000-word background paper issued simultaneously by the Office of the White House Press Secretary.

3. S.2963 also placed substantial limits on the circulation of conviction records.

terminals maintained by law enforcement agencies in the various states, Typically, NCIC works like this: a policeman spots a car which arouses his suspicions; he radios its license number to headquarters, which in turn feeds the number into a computer and learns from NCIC whether it has been stolen; the policeman will be told in minutes whether the car is wanted, even if in a state halfway across the country. The Justice Department Annual Report for 1972 says there were some 90,000 such transactions involving NCIC every day, of which about 750 resulted in positive responses. That leaves some 89,250 transactions a day which resulted in negative responses, which doesn't say a great deal for the intuitive suspicions of the nation's police.

In general, the records stored in NCIC are more accurate and more complete than those maintained in the much larger Identification Division, and they are less widely disseminated. But because it is computerized, NCIC has inspired far greater fears than the Identification Division, a manual system operating through the U.S. mails.

In 1973, the Commonwealth of Massachusetts decided that, because the restrictions on the dissemination of records by NCIC were inadequate, the state would no longer forward arrest data to the FBI. The state's action caused a sensation and led to a Justice Department suit against the state, quashed by Elliot Richardson during his brief tenure as attorney general. The Massachusetts episode added to the public interest in the arrest records issue and helped set the stage for Senate hearings on S.2963 and S.2964 in March 1974.

At the hearings, it turned out that the Nixon administration's support for its own bill, S.2964, was less than wholehearted. Although the bill had been drafted by its parent body, the Justice Department, the FBI came to the hearings to testify against the bill, a development I believe to be unprecedented. Prohibitions on dissemination of arrest records did gain support from other quarters. It is an idea whose time will soon come. The American Bankers Association, a powerful and conservative institution representing 96 percent of the country's 14,000 banks, went on record at the hearings in support of prohibitions on the dissemination of records of arrests not followed by convictions. "While all lawyers recognize," said the bankers, "that those who have committed crimes are not always prosecuted, or even if prosecuted, are not always convicted, and while the presumption that a person is presumed innocent until proven guilty does not qualify him for a sensitive position of trust—for work in a bank or for that matter for admission to the bar—the presumption is sufficiently strong and sufficiently valid to serve as the basis for withholding arrest records." The issue is being seriously considered in other forums, as well. Two United States Courts of Appeals have found that questions about arrest records are racially discriminatory. Citing these court decisions, the New York City Commission on Human Rights issued "guidelines" on January 4, 1973, stating that "it will be considered an unlawful discriminatory practice for employers or employment agencies to ask of any applicant or employee any questions relating to arrest records" or to solicit the information from another source.

The guidelines of the City Commission on Human Rights grew out of several days of hearings in 1972 on employment difficulties faced by people with arrest records and people with conviction records. Those hearings were, in part, a result of the commission's earlier hearings on the employment practices of the Board of Examiners of the New York City Board of Education, which licenses teachers for the New York City public schools. There was testimony at the hearings about the denial of teacher licenses to people arrested in civil-rights demonstrations in Mississippi. In another Board of Examiners case, a young man, David Mills (not his real name), who had been convicted of a misdemeanor in New York City Criminal Court, applied for a license as a substitute teacher in the public schools. A few months later, in May 1970, he was summoned before the Board of Examiners to explain the circumstances of his conviction, then on appeal. He was assured by two examining officers that if the conviction was reversed, he would have no difficulty getting a license.

The Appellate Court unanimously reversed Mills's conviction "on the law and the facts." Mills immediately took a copy of the decision to the Board of Examiners. The runaround began. Even though he had taken the license examination the previous February, he was told for the first time that he now needed a "nomination" from a specific high school that wished to employ him. Next, he learned that his application had to be approved by the Board of Education's Department of Personnel. After the Department of Personnel finally approved the license, the Board of Examiners still refused to issue it, claiming more time was needed to investigate Mills's "criminal" record. With delay piled upon delay, Mills filed suit against the Board of Examiners to compel it to issue the license. In the face of the lawsuit, the Board of Examiners caved in and granted Mills his license.

The first court decision that inquiries about arrest records are racially discriminatory came in *Gregory v. Litton Systems,* a case brought by the American Civil Liberties Union of Southern California. Earl Gregory, a Los Angeles black, seemed an unlikely candidate for a test case. He had a record of no fewer than fourteen arrests. Gregory had sought a job as a sheet-metal mechanic. Although he was qualified, he was turned down because "Litton's standard policy," it was said in court, "is not to hire applicants who have been arrested on a number of occasions beyond minor traffic offenses."

Gregory's arrest record was not unusual. Dr. Ronald Christensen, one of the authors of the Report of the President's Law Enforcement Commission, who appeared as a witness, testified that a person who has been arrested once tends to accumulate additional arrests during his lifetime. The average number of arrests for a white man once arrested is 7; for a black man the lifetime average is 12½. Christensen and another prominent analyst of crime statistics, Dr. Marvin Wolfgang, testified that in one large category of arrests—on "suspicion" or for "investigation"—blacks are arrested about four times as often as whites. Dr. Wolfgang pointed to a study of "investigation" arrests in 1964 in Baltimore; 98 percent of the persons arrested had been released without further proceedings. The court heard extensive testimony that persons who had been arrested on a number of occasions performed as efficiently and honestly on the job as persons who had never been arrested.

Litton Systems argued that the "business justification for considering a person's arrest record in determining whether or not to hire him is the same as considering a record of conviction. . . . It is not a fact, and it cannot be assumed, that all arrests which did not result in conviction are unfounded." The testimony by Christensen and Wolfgang proved to Litton "that people with arrest records are arrest prone, and that the proneness increases with the number of prior arrests. There is business justification in declining to hire people with arrest records because the employer has a legitimate reason in not wanting to hire people who are more likely to be absent when they are arrested. . . ." While Litton cited no other "business justifications," the firm expressed a certain pique that it was being singled out for attack. An inquiry about arrest records, Litton told the court, "is one of the most common employment practices known to man. Almost anyone who has ever applied for a job has answered this type of question . . . the employer who does not obtain and utilize arrest information in determining whether or not to hire is the exception, not the rule."

Litton's arguments about employers' reliance on arrest records are supported by a February 1972 report issued by the Georgetown University Law Center, prepared under a grant from the U.S. Department of Labor. It found that "the existence of arrest records is all-pervasive in our society and that millions of individuals may be hampered in their efforts at finding jobs and pursuing careers because of such records." Most state and county governments inquire about such records on job-application forms. Sometimes arrest records are absolute barriers to public employment, the report says; commonly they restrict applicants who are hired to low-skill jobs.

In its first decision in the Dale Menard case, the U.S. Court of Appeals in the District of Columbia referred to another study showing that 75 percent of the employment agencies in the New York area will not accept for referral applicants with arrest records. In another survey, sixty-six of seventy-five employers would refuse to consider hiring a man who had been arrested for assault even though he had been acquitted.

The fact that Litton's policies were no worse than those of other employers did not deter the federal court. It awarded to Earl Gregory $4,400 in damages because of the inquiry about his arrest record. In February 1973, that judgment was upheld by the U.S. Court of Appeals in California.

One of the most sweeping actions against arrest records was a recent decision by the Supreme Court of Colorado. The court ruled that arrest records of persons not convicted must be expunged unless the police can demonstrate the need to keep the record.

Dorothy Davidson, executive director of the Colorado ACLU, was the plaintiff in the suit. She had been arrested in 1968 while trying to act as an observer at a police-hippie confrontation in Denver. (These arrests are an occupational hazard for local ACLU directors. In 1968, there were similar arrests in four other states. I was the director of the New York CLU at the time and was arrested while observing an antiwar demonstration in Manhattan's Washington Square Park. None of us were convicted.) The court found expungement of arrest records necessary because "the record here is devoid of any facts showing . . . the ability of the [Denver police] department to keep them confidential." The Colorado Supreme Court decision brings to mind the passage in Franz Kafka's *The Trial* in which the painter Titorelli explains to Joseph K. the distinction between definite acquittal and ostensible acquittal. "In definite acquittal," says Titorelli, "the documents relating to the case are said to be completely annulled, they simply vanish from sight, not only the charge but also the records of the case and even the acquittal are destroyed, everything is destroyed. That's not the case with ostensible acquittal. The documents remain as they were. . . . The whole dossier continues to circulate as the regular official routine demands. . . ."

Only expungement or "definite acquittal," in Kafka's words, can possibly keep arrest records confidential. The New York State Identification and Intelligence System was established in 1964. It was not supposed to be available for private-employment checks. Five years later the state legislature passed a law requiring the fingerprinting of all employees in the securities industry, one of the state's largest. Prints are now checked against the six million on file with NYSIIS, and the information is given to the state attorney general, who, in turn, makes it available to the employers. In his first report on the program, New York Attorney General Louis Lefkowitz announced with great pride that several hundred employees had been discovered to have "criminal records" and that many had been fired. About half of those fired had no record of convictions, only of arrests. A federal district court dismissed the New York Civil Liberties Union challenge to the fingerprinting and the decision was upheld on appeal.

If one member of a family has been arrested, it can cause trouble for another member of the family. Norma Winters (not her real name) was asked for information about arrests of members of her family when she applied to become a New York policewoman. Winters responded that her husband had been arrested four years previously for drug possession and had been released on condition that he enter a treatment program. In a hearing before three captains, she was asked whether if she had a gun in the house, her husband might be tempted to take it and rob someone. The panel conceded that her own record was good and that she was qualified for the Police Department. Because of her husband's record, the panel ruled against her 2–1.

An arrest record in the family can mean expulsion from public housing. Mildred Brown has lived in a housing project on Manhattan's East Side for twenty years. A finding of the New York City Housing Authority that she was "ineligible for continued occupancy on the ground of nondesirability" was based in large part on her son's arrest record. Ms. Brown's experience is common.

Arrest records affect chances for admission to educational institutions, opportunities for financial credit, and, as Litton's arguments about "arrest-prone" people suggest, they increase the likelihood of rearrest. A young black man in Washington, D.C., recently filed suit to stop police harassment. In his senior year in high school he had been arrested on a robbery charge; he was acquitted because of an apparent case of mistaken identity. He is now a college student and a National Merit Scholarship winner. According to his court complaint, on at least three occasions police have shown his photograph in neighborhoods where crimes have been committed, seeking to have him identified as the criminal in some new crime. Each time this has been done, his family and friends have been interrogated anew.

People with arrest records are natural targets for investigation when new crimes are committed. Inevitably, further arrests follow. Being "arrest-prone," therefore, is often simply a result of having been arrested before. The practice is to "round up the usual suspects," as police Captain Louis Renault (played by Claude Rains) put it in the film "Casablanca."

There is no indication that the FBI gives any arrest information directly to a credit bureau; nevertheless, the FBI has been notoriously loose in policing the further distribution of the records it disseminates. Here is the testimony of Special Agent Ponder at the Menard trial:

Q. Is there any procedure whereby the FBI or any division of the FBI inquiries into the uses to which the arrest information is put by contributing agencies?

A. No.

Q. Are any restrictions imposed by the FBI on the use to which that information is put?

A. Yes. Official business only.

Q. Are there memoranda or orders indicating that there is a restriction?

A. It is right on the record itself.

Q. Are there any form letters that are sent to contributing agencies explaining what "official business only" means?

A. Well, in years gone by we have brought this to the attention of contributors, that this information is disseminated strictly for official use only.

After Ponder was questioned on December 17, 1970, he supplied for the court record the FBI's most recent notice on the issue, a memorandum of October 18, 1965, from the late J. Edgar Hoover. If the records were used for other than "official uses," Hoover warned, "this service is subject to cancellation." No other penalty was mentioned.

Judicial and legislative action to control the use and distribution of arrest records will have little impact for a long time to come. The records of people arrested in the past have often been so widely circulated that it will be almost impossible to prevent them from haunting their victims for years to come. But action has to start sometime. There is even a small sign that the FBI is concerned. In 1973 the FBI announced it had "purged inactive arrest records of individuals age 80 and older from the fingerprint files." A lot of octogenarians out looking for jobs will be very grateful.

9

The Scarlet Letter

CONVICTION RECORDS

When Thomas Carr was a teen-ager, he was arrested and convicted of some minor offenses: petty larceny, disorderly conduct, and escaping arrest. His last conviction for a nontraffic offense came when he was twenty years old. A decade later, in 1972, he applied for work for the City of Niagara Falls as an assistant filter operator. The Niagara Falls Civil Service Commission barred Carr from taking the required exam. Because of his criminal record, they said, he did not come up to the standards for civil service employees: "Good moral character and habits and a satisfactory reputation." Unable to get a job in New York, Carr moved to another state.

Because John Huff was a truant from junior high school in Baltimore, he was committed to a Maryland state training school. He got out at seventeen, and soon afterward was convicted of armed robbery for using a knife to try to rob two men who gave him a lift in their car. He went to prison for eighteen months. When his term was over, he went to the State Employment Service for a job. He listened while the employment counselor explained on the phone to people looking for help that Huff had been convicted of armed robbery. No one would even give him an interview.

With no job or hope of one, Huff resorted to burglaries and was caught again. In prison, he became a skilled welder. When he got out, he took the test to become a welder at a shipyard and passed, but failed the physical, or so the shipyard told him. "There's always some excuse like that they find," he says.

Theodore Miller learned how to make jewelry in the arts and crafts program in the District of Columbia's Lorton prison. After he served his time, he applied for a license to be a street vendor of his own jewelry. The District of Columbia Department of Economic Development turned down the application because of Miller's record going back to his teens. He got the license later but only after the D.C. Court of Appeals ordered it. The decision was not based on the injustice of continuing punishment but on the technicality that the Economic Development Department had acted in the absence of formal guidelines.

The President's Commission on Law Enforcement, in a study of conviction records, found that 19 percent of all males and 25 percent of all urban males will be convicted at some time during their lives; 5 percent of all females will acquire conviction records.[1]

Thirty-seven percent of paroled federal prisoners had part-time jobs or no jobs at all according to a 1969 study by the U.S. Department of Labor, *Employment Problems of Released Prisoners*. This was about triple the rate of full or partial unemployment nationally. Exconvicts not on parole probably have even a harder time getting a job than paroled federal prisoners. Since parole may require employment of some sort, no matter how menial, parole authorities may offer some slight aid to prisoners in obtaining jobs. Also, federal parolees are more employable than individuals who have left state prisons. Many of the inmates of federal prisons in the 1960s, when the Labor Department did its study, were there for violations of the draft

---

1. The commission was more tentative in calculating conviction statistics than those on arrest because of limitations on the data available. The commission did not attempt to categorize conviction statistics by race.

laws, others for income tax violation, securities law infractions, mail fraud, and car theft.[2] Most of those in state prison systems have been convicted of murder, rape, robbery, assault, burglary, and various drug offenses. The kinds of crimes of which they have been convicted inspire the greatest fear among potential employers. These men have fewer legitimate job skills.

The government that has convicted, sentenced and then released a person proceeds to make the chances of new crimes more likely. A man without a job can be a desperate man. In more than half the states, public employment is flatly closed to persons with criminal convictions. Almost all other states consider conviction records when hiring. Most of the more than ten million jobs in state and local government are closed to exconvicts by these laws and practices.

Until very recently, persons convicted of felonies could not fill Federal Civil Service jobs for two years after they had completed their sentences, and those convicted of misdemeanors had to wait one year. This policy denied the exconvict a job during the decisive period when he must either rehabilitate himself through a job or go back to the life that led him to crime. A relaxation of this policy is now underway. The old rules were described in a July 1974 newsletter published by a unit of the American Bar Association as "generalized guidelines." Thomas P. Sandow, chief of the Division of Adjudication and Appraisal in the Civil Service Commission's Bureau of Personnel Investigations, said the guidelines were "subject to as liberal an interpretation as the general mood of the public might happen to be."

Exconvicts are barred from many jobs with private employers, as well. Defense Department rules prohibit contractors from employing persons with criminal records in many jobs. The Labor Management Reporting and Disclosure Act denies felons the right to serve as labor union officials. A federal law bars persons con-

2. Car theft is a federal crime when the cars are taken across state lines.

victed of many kinds of crimes from working for institutions that are members of the Federal Deposit Insurance Corporation.

Many state laws governing licensing of lawyers, teachers, fortune tellers, masseurs, junk dealers, dry cleaners, barbers, plumbers, taxi drivers, and almost anything else that the state legislatures have seen fit to supervise deny licenses to exconvicts. The American Bar Association found that 1,948 of the state statutory provisions on licensing turn away exconvicts.[3] (Some seven million persons work in directly licensed occupations and, in New York City alone, about 500,000 jobs are controlled by licensing laws.)

The licensing laws produce bizarre results. Men trained in prison as barbers are unable to get licenses to become barbers when they get out of prison because of licensing law restrictions. The laws of forty-six states and the District of Columbia deny licenses as barbers to persons who have been convicted of crime. That particular restriction may be explicable (if not justifiable) by the fear of allowing exconvicts to hold jobs in which the straight-razor is a principal tool of the trade! Exconvicts are also denied the right to become cosmetologist/beauticians—a trade in which about 485,000 people are employed—in forty-seven states and the District of Columbia.

Many states deny drivers licenses to persons convicted of felonies. A salesman, truck driver, or ambulance attendant needs a driver's license.

Many states prohibit the employment of exconvicts where liquor is sold. An exconvict may be denied a job as a produce clerk in a supermarket that has a license to sell beer, as a dishwasher in a restaurant, or as a laundry room employee in a hotel, or he may get the job only when the state liquor agency gives specific ap-

3. *Laws, Licenses and the Offender's Right to Work,* published by the ABA's National Clearinghouse on Offender Employment Restrictions, Washington, D.C., 1973. Some of these statutes (134) simply bar issuance of a license to an exconvict; but most require vague conditions—707 deny a license to a person who has committed a crime or who does not possess "good moral character," and the rest just specify "good moral character" and that is generally interpreted to mean no criminal conviction, an interpretation that has been sustained by the courts.

proval. Several million jobs are closed to exconvicts by these indirect consequences of licensing laws.

Jerome D. Peterson worked as a porter, cleaning floors and windows, emptying trash, and refilling water coolers, after his release from prison in 1954. He had been convicted of assault in 1949 when he was twenty-four years old and served the full five years of his sentence in Attica. In 1969, three years after Peterson started work at the Fisherman's Wharf tavern in Buffalo, his employer found out that the New York Alcoholic Beverage Control Law requires exfelons to get the State Liquor Authority's approval for work in licensed premises. Peterson applied and was turned down even though twenty years had elapsed since his felony conviction and even though his most serious nontraffic offense in the intervening period had resulted in a $15.00 fine. Peterson lost his job.

Two years later, unable to find a different kind of a job, Peterson again sought the State Liquor Authority's approval for work as a porter in a tavern. The application was summarily denied. After a third application also was refused, the matter was taken to court by Herman Schwartz, a professor of law at the State University of New York in Buffalo, acting for the New York Civil Liberties Union. Schwartz, who has pioneered the effort to win rights for prisoners, won a court decision that held the State Liquor Authority's actions to be arbitrary and capricious. The decision was appealed by New York State and the appellate court remanded the case to the Liquor Authority. In the fall of 1973, under court pressure, the Liquor Authority allowed Peterson to go back to work for Fisherman's Wharf. As Schwartz has written to me, "The sad thing about it is that but for the fact that Peterson somehow managed to interest one of my students in his case, he would still be without this job."

Conviction records, of all the kinds of records discussed in this book, have the greatest probative value, that is, they are more reasonable. Unlike arrest records, which are merely allegations, often entirely unfounded and, at the very least, unsubstantiated, conviction records result from proof of guilt beyond a reasonable doubt or, more often, admission of guilt. There is nevertheless a strong argument, rooted in the concept of due process of law, that the dissemination of conviction records should be forbidden. The argument was made by a one-time inmate of Attica prison. "Once you have a 'jacket,' a dossier with all the past details of your life, all the detrimental ones they can put together, that is," he wrote, "you are a *criminal*. The jacket does not disappear, it grows fat and follows you around wherever you go. Someday this sentence you are serving will chronologically run out, but Society does not forgive; it keeps tabs. . . ." [4]

Our laws provide fixed penalties for crimes. The maximum penalty for any crime should be that fixed in the criminal law, and no more. Distribution of conviction records makes a penalty life-long and, I believe, violates due process.

Before due process was incorporated in our Constitution, crimes were often punished by a deliberate effort to stigmatize the miscreant for life. The adultress was condemned to wear the scarlet letter A. Other criminals were branded on the thumb or had part of their ears clipped off to advise all with whom they came in contact of their crimes. Such barbarous practice of public shame ended when an effort at salvation replaced it. Prisons became popular in the 1820s and 1830s, in the reformist mood of the Jacksonian period, as a way of isolating the criminal from the corrupting influence of his environment so that he could be reha-bilitated. The prisoner was expected to acquire good work habits inside the prison. After his release he was expected to live in society as a self-supporting and respectable citizen.[5]

Alexis de Tocqueville and his friend and fellow traveler in America, Gustave de Beaumont, visited Syracuse, New York, in

4. William R. Coons, "An Attica Graduate Tells His Story," *New York Times Maga-zine*, October 10, 1971.

5. See David J. Rothman, *The Discovery of the Asylum* (Boston: Little, Brown, 1971).

1831 to interview Elam Lynds, the builder of Sing Sing and warden of Auburn Prison. De Tocqueville recorded the conversation:

Q. Do you at bottom believe in the *reform* of a great number of the
inmates?

A. We must understand each other. I do not believe in complete
reform (except for juvenile delinquents), that is to say, I do not think that
one has often seen a mature criminal become a religious and virtuous
man. I don't have any faith in the saintliness of those who leave prison,
and I don't believe that the exhortations of the chaplain or the private
reflections of the inmate ever make a good Christian of him. But my
opinion is that a great number of former convicts do not relapse into
crime, and they even become useful citizens, having learned a trade in
prison and acquired the habit of steady work. This is the only reform that
I have ever hoped to produce, and I think it's the only one which society
can demand.[6]

At Auburn, De Tocqueville and Beaumont saw a comb shop,
stonecutting shop, tool shop, shoemaker's shop, cooper's shop,
weaver's shop, and blacksmith's shop. Rehabilitation through
work was to lead ultimately to useful work outside its walls.

Contemporary prisons and "correctional" programs are still
rooted in the theories of the Jacksonian period. Convicts are in
institutions which cut them off from society. They are placed on a
work regimen, designed as the American Correctional Association's *Manual of Correctional Standards* says, because "the principal value of work activity is to be found in the opportunity it
may afford for the inculcation, or the reactivation, of attitudes,
skills and habit patterns which can be instrumental in the rehabilitation of many offenders."

Work, rather than the money earned for it, is expected to
rehabilitate prisoners. When wages are paid for prison labor, they

6. Quoted in George Wilson Pierson, *Tocqueville in America* (Garden City, New York:
Doubleday-Anchor, 1959), pp. 130–131.

only provide meager sums to spend at the prison commissary on cigarettes, candy, and magazines. The five cents to twenty cents an hour that is standard pay for prisoners permits no savings to use once they get out. Isolation and tedious work at demeaning pay are not conducive to rehabilitation.

The prisoner is expected to be able to fend for himself once released. He hasn't, of course, been able to save money while in prison and, in all probability, he has no bank account waiting for him when he gets out. The prisoner who has been released must rely on what he can earn—that and the $40 or $50 that is given to him to hold him until he collects his first paycheck.

A black exconvict, Joseph McAfee, testifying on January 29, 1972, before a subcommittee of the House of Representatives Judiciary Committee, told what happens: "So the ex-convict runs from [employment] agency to agency and he becomes discouraged," said McAfee. "Remember he has only $50 when he gets out, out of which he has to pay rent, he has to buy clothing, he has to start from scratch with nothing . . . he becomes disillusioned when door after door is closed in his face. . . . So he takes his last $12 and he buys a gun. This is his last resort because nobody is going to sit by and starve in this land of plenty . . ."

Behind bars, prisoners may have lost friends and contacts. Many prisoners are unskilled and some of the skills learned in prison—manufacturing license plates and sewing mail bags—cannot be readily translated into civilian employment. But above all else, there is the record, the contemporary equivalent of the scarlet A. Joseph McAfee testified about the prospects for a prisoner who did acquire skills in prison but who would still find the record in his way: "Now I am not using Caterpillar Tractor Co., as an example," he said, "but just as a hypothetical situation. Caterpillar Tractor Co. has taken its obsolete machinery, donated it to the State of Illinois and then they get a tax write-off, and an ex-offender turns around after he has been trained on that machinery, and he goes for a job interview and can't get a job. You know who would be the first one I would want to stickup, would be the president of Caterpillar Tractor Co., and the next guy would be the guy that let him get the tax write-off."

Former Attorney General John Mitchell, hardly noted for his civil-libertarian zeal, told a National Conference on Corrections in December 1971 about "an appalling resistance to hiring ex-offenders, even by many government agencies at different levels. . . . When the releasee is thus denied the means of making an honest living," said Mitchell, "every sentence becomes a life sentence."

It probably did not occur to Mitchell that he, along with some of his closest associates, might someday themselves face employment difficulties because of criminal records.

Some progress is being made. The most sweeping reform was enacted by Hawaii in mid-1974. Under an amendment to the state's Fair Employment Practice Law, job discrimination against exconvicts is just as illegal as discrimination based on race or sex unless the employer proves that a specific job requires discriminatory selection or the applicant's crime is directly relevant to the job sought.

A 1967 California law bars public agencies from denying licenses to exconvicts trained to qualify for the license while in prison. In 1972, New York's Alcohol Beverage Control Law was changed to allow exconvicts to be employed in liquor stores. In 1972, Montana adopted a state constitutional provision to permit restoration of full rights to employment upon the completion of a criminal sentence. And, in that same year, the governor of Maine ordered state agencies not to deny jobs to applicants because of prior criminal records. Several other states have taken baby steps in this direction. The courts, so far, have seldom been willing to strike down job discrimination based on criminal records. In coming years they will undoubtedly face a great deal of litigation on this problem. The legal attack will focus on the racially discriminatory impact of denying employment because of conviction records and on the failure to show a direct relationship between convictions for certain crimes and the jobs denied.

Even if jobs were widely available to exconvicts, it would not be easy to reenter society. David Rothenberg, the founder of the Fortune Society, has described what the world is like to the exconvict freed after a long period behind bars: "There are people who do not know how to ride the subways, get on a bus, order a meal from a menu, put on a television set, dial a phone," said Rothenberg. "They must slowly learn how to function, and this with Parole pressuring them to find a job and with the necessities of economic survival dictating their pursuit of alien patterns. They are confronted by housing, welfare, educational and vocational choices that stagger their senses and terrify them at every turn." [7]

Halfway houses and work-release programs have proven to be modestly successful in assisting the transition to freedom. However, these programs meet great resistance from communities fearful of being chosen as the sites for halfway houses or of having prisoners who sleep in prison at night move freely among them during the working day. Whatever the successes in the gradual reintegration of prisoners into society, these programs have not persuaded large numbers of public or private employers to relax the restrictions they have imposed on employment of exconvicts. Criminal convictions remain life sentences, no matter what the penalties provided by law. The dossiers that impose these sentences follow the formerly convicted everywhere all of their lives. In the name of protecting society, they compel many desperate men and women to choose a life of crime.

7. *Prisoner's Rights Sourcebook*, edited by Michele G. Hermann and Marilyn G. Haft (New York: Clark Boardman, 1973), p. 534.

10

Modus Inoperandi

THE FBI FILES

Arrest records have served to assist law enforcement authorities in the solution of many cases. They provide leads to suspects, knowledge of the whereabouts of other individuals who can thus be eliminated as suspects and, as a result, save valuable time and energy.

That is the way Clarence Kelley, director of the FBI, put it during the course of Senate testimony on March 7, 1974. The claim that arrest dossiers serve a critical role in the control of crime has gone virtually unchallenged. Even those who support limits on circulation of such records tend to accept the proposition that the records are a valuable investigative tool while they contend that the benefits of law enforcement do not justify the damage to those whose arrest records are disseminated. The outcome of a debate framed in those terms seems inevitable. Americans are not willing to deprive law enforcement agencies of a crucial investigative tool.

In fact, how valuable *are* arrest records—or even conviction records, for that matter—in investigating crime? From what I have been able to gather, investigation of crime is the least significant use that has been made of such records during the past fifty years. Indeed, if the hundreds of millions of dollars presently spent by federal, state, and local agencies on the maintenance and dissemination of records were devoted to other law enforcement uses, the capacity to deter and investigate crime would be increased.

When law enforcement officials talk about the value of records in investigations, sooner or later they use the term *modus operandi*, meaning the mode of operation that criminals follow in committing crimes. By studying the patterns they followed in the past, investigators hope to locate the perpetrator of some new offense.

In his March 1974 Senate testimony, Kelley attempted to give the impression that this is the investigative purpose served by the FBI's giant fingerprint files. "An examination of past criminal records," said Kelley, "can produce information which reflects that one or more suspects have been involved in similar criminal activity. This could narrow the investigation and would lead to a detailed examination of their *modus operandi. . . .*"

In the leading court case on the FBI's arrest record files, *Menard v. Mitchell*, Judge Gerhard Gesell invited the Bureau to prove the point. "I would like to hear testimony," said Gesell, "if there is such, which would indicate or relate to the points the Court has been discussing earlier today. My impression as to how law enforcement operates may be erroneous, but I had always thought that the assembling of bits and pieces of factual information could often be successfully interrelated to assist in the apprehension of . . . guilty persons. I would imagine that the Bureau's experience is simply replete with examples of that. . . . I have had a feeling that much of this data . . . may have considerable value in terms of the law-enforcing function, in assisting in the location of people, in assisting in getting information about the *modus operandi* of different individuals, and so forth."

Despite Gesell's request and despite more than 250 pages of testimony from the chief of the FBI's Identification Division, Beverly Ponder, no evidence was presented to show that the files were used or could be used for investigative purposes.

No such testimony emerged because the FBI's files are not organized according to *modus operandi*. They are organized by fingerprints which, the Bureau insists, are the only reliable means of matching a suspect to existing records.

FBI publications generally make the case for the use of fingerprints to identify people by telling the story of Will West. As a new prisoner, West was brought into an office at Leavenworth Penitentiary one day in 1903 to be photographed and measured for the Bertillon system. This method of criminal identification, devised in the 1880s by a Frenchman, Alphonse Bertillon, involved a series of measurements of the body such as head, arm, foot, and finger. The measurements and the photographs were part of an identification file. Since it was thought that no two people could have both the same appearance and the same measurements, the Bertillon system was regarded as absolutely reliable.

The Will West incident changed all that. On file at Leavenworth was a card for a William West. The photograph and measurements were an excellent fit for the Will West in the prison office at that moment. There was only one problem: the card referred to a William West already in a cell elsewhere in Leavenworth serving out a life sentence.

When a person is arrested and booked, his fingerprints are forwarded to the FBI. If the prints were not previously in the FBI's files, they are added. If they were already on file, the information on the new arrest is inserted, and the agency that submitted the prints gets back from the FBI the person's previous arrest record. If the FBI has the information (which is unlikely), the dispositions of those arrests are also sent.

The person's past record may be useful to a judge who is making a decision about bail, but bail is generally set within a matter of hours, or at most a day or two after arrest. The FBI's giant Identification Division, which has operated manually through the mails, isn't much help, though this may change with computerization. If the person should be convicted on the new charges, the past record may be helpful to a judge pondering sentence.

Law enforcement agencies argue for the maintenance and dissemination of fingerprint records on the ground of compelling public concern—investigative practices that solve crimes. But since the files are only consulted *after* a person has been arrested and fingerprinted, it is an argument without much merit.

Our laws require that arrests be preceded by probable cause to believe a particular person has committed a particular crime. Dragnet arrests are unconstitutional. We do not tolerate mass roundups. Before an arrest may be made, an investigation must be virtually complete and probable cause must be found. Information received after arrest and fingerprinting is a lot less significant than it would be if all the talk about *modus operandi* were supported in practice.

Then what purpose is served by the FBI's fingerprint files? They are used, of course, when police take fingerprints at the scene of a crime and send them to the bureau to try to determine who committed a particular crime. This sort of thing happens often in the movies, but as anyone who has ever been the victim of an assault, a burglary, or a robbery knows, the investigation is rarely done with magnifying glass and dusting powder.

The real life way in which police investigate crime is described in a comprehensive study of robbery arrests by the Oakland Police Department. The report by the Center on Administration of Criminal Justice of the University of California on "The Prevention and Control of Robbery" was financed with grants from the Ford Foundation and the Department of Justice and published in February 1974.

Robbery is a major crime involving the threat of serious physical harm to the victim. Murders which do not result from fights between friends, relatives, and acquaintances are often the result of robbery. The FBI says that robbery accounts for 48 percent of all crimes of violence. Therefore, it would seem appropriate to test the value of criminal-offender records in police investigations in robbery cases.

Investigative efforts played only a minor role in catching robbery suspects in Oakland. "Studies undertaken in several cities," the report notes, "indicate that between 70 and 90 percent of all robbery arrests are made by patrol units." Either a patrol unit surprises the robbers in the act or it gives chase after an immediate outcry or a victim recognizes a robber later and informs patrolling police.

Identification of the robber is critical in arresting suspects. In Oakland, "Fifty-eight percent of all identifications were by the victim, 38 percent by a witness, and the remaining 4 percent by a crime partner. Most positive identifications were made on the street within one hour of the crime," according to the study. "Selected mug shots were the next best source of positive identifications and lineups were rarely a source of positive identifications and were used only as a last resort. In a total of 225 identification attempts made for the sample studied, 122 were on-scene identifications. There were 41 identification attempts utilizing mug shots and 36 lineups. Of the 55 instances in which there was no positive identification, 27 involved lineups, 14 mug shots and 14 field identifications."

In this description of a typical urban police department's efforts to identify robbery suspects, there is no mention at all of consulting the FBI's fingerprint files.

Fingerprints left behind at the scene of a crime are not easily identified. "Classifying fingerprints is child's play," says noted police scientist, Jay Cameron Hall. "Finding and raising latent prints at crime scenes is another matter . . . latents are usually forgotten unless the importance of the case calls for heroic measures." [1]

The public image of police investigation tends to be shaped

1. Jay Cameron Hall, *Inside the Crime Lab* (Englewood Cliffs, N.J.: Prentice-Hall, 1973), pp. 157–158.

precisely by those cases which call for "heroic measures" and attract the attention of the news media: the kidnapping of Patricia Hearst, the murders of Janice Wylie and Emily Hoffert, the theft of jewels from New York's Museum of Natural History, or the robbery at the Pierre Hotel. Just because such cases are so visible, law enforcement agencies will expend tremendous effort on them, up to and including an effort to identify fingerprints. The ordinary robberies of the sort studied in Oakland and the ordinary burglaries, robberies, assaults, rapes, and murders which make up the crime problem that frightens so many Americans are just not dealt with in the same way.

Even if a single fingerprint left at the scene of a crime can be raised, it is usually insufficient to identify the culprit. Many thousands of people may have single prints which look identical. Hall points out that "before standard ten-print files are useful for latent print identification, the researcher must have a specific suspect in mind. Only then can his or her card be compared with evidence fingerprints."

Let us concede for a moment an unlikely proposition: that the expenditure of people, time, and money on the operations of the FBI Identification Division can be justified by the identifications made in a few big cases when latent prints are available and suspects have already been identified though not yet with sufficient certainty to permit prosecution. All this would only justify a fingerprint bank. There would be no excuse for the dissemination of 29,000 reports a day to agencies that have obtained fingerprints from people who are already in police custody or who have given their prints when they applied for jobs or licenses.

The intertwining of the police laboratory and credit bureau functions performed by the Identification Division enabled the FBI to accumulate some 200 million fingerprint cards. While many are duplicates, and others are of people long dead, the fingerprints of the majority of living adult males are presently on file. The collection could not have been built unless a great many public and private agencies had the incentive to send fingerprint cards to the FBI. Getting back data for use in employment and licensing decisions provides the incentive.

The FBI's files could be said to serve an investigative purpose in one other way. When a person is arrested in connection with one crime, a check with the FBI may disclose that the same person is wanted elsewhere. Other more accidental contacts with police may result in the arrest of a fugitive, as Robert C. Daly recently discovered. Daly was employed painting a bridge over Chesapeake Bay in Maryland when he fell off a scaffolding and had to be fished out of the water. A partner drowned. Maryland state police took Daly to a hospital and then checked him with the FBI's computerized National Crime Information Center through MILES, the Maryland Interagency Law Enforcement System. NCIC reported that Daly was wanted in Georgia on forgery charges. He was arrested and returned to Georgia to stand trial.

In the books written over the years in glorification of the FBI, the stories chosen to illustrate the value of the bureau's Identification Division generally seem to be similar to the case of Robert Daly. One of the earliest books in this genre was an autobiographical account by the well-known FBI agent, Melvin H. Purvis, himself once the director of the Identification Division. Purvis was enthusiastic about the exchange of fingerprints. "There is one incident, however, that I cannot resist telling," he wrote. "There was a calamitous fire at the Ohio State Penitentiary during 1930. More than a hundred men were burned to death and it was believed that one of them was a certain Elmer Whiting. In September of 1932 a man named Jerry Cobern was arrested at Mishawaka, Indiana. His fingerprints arrived in Washington. There it was discovered that they matched precisely with those of Elmer Whiting, the unfortunate who supposedly had died in the Columbus holocaust. Then the truth came out: Whiting had escaped in the confusion and excitement which accompanied the fire; for two years he had been free. He was returned to the penitentiary to finish his term." [2]

Writing about the FBI during World War II, John Floherty illustrated the value of the Identification Division by describing what happened to a John Davis who enlisted in the U.S. Army: "A search of the fingerprint files," said Floherty, "showed that Davis' fingerprint card had a red tab attached to it—the danger signal indicating that he was a fugitive. Further examination showed that he was wanted as a parole violator in New York. . . . Upon establishing Davis' identity, the FBI notified the Army and the New York authorities." [3]

Floherty noted that, "Before the advent of fingerprinting the army and navy were favorite hiding places of criminals and fugitives from justice." [4]

The most popular book on the bureau's work, Don Whitehead's *The FBI Story,*[5] recounted a series of eight incidents designed to demonstrate the value of fingerprints. None of them involved *modus operandi* investigations. In one, a man wanted for murder in Colorado was located when the fingerprints of a man arrested in Oklahoma for robbery were sent to the FBI. In a second a "notor-

2. Melvin H. Purvis, *American Agent* (New York: Garden City Publishing Company, 1938), pp. 68–69.

3. John F. Floherty, *Inside the FBI* (Philadelphia: J.B. Lippincott Company, 1943), p. 27. This book, which contained an introduction by J. Edgar Hoover, was perhaps the most unabashed of them all in praising everything about the bureau. It contained this portrait of the director:

> Of the 13,000 people employed in the FBI the director is the hardest worker. Now in his late forties, he is as rugged as some of his men who are only half his age. When things are quiet his office hours are from eight-thirty in the morning until seven-thirty at night, every minute crammed with high speed activity. When he is on a case he often goes without sleep for forty-eight hours and has been known on many occasions to have gone seventy-two hours without as much as a nap, and with nothing to eat but a few sandwiches. In spite of these physical strains, he keeps in the pink of condition with moderate living. Yet with all the seriousness of his job, he is jovial and full of the joy of life. (p. 18.)

4. Ibid., p. 27.

5. (New York: Random House, 1956).

ious" narcotics peddler in San Francisco was cleared because the FBI reported that the print on an envelope containing heroin was not his.[6] In a third a Tennessee police department tried to trick the FBI into believing that a photograph of a suspect's fingerprint taken after arrest was actually a photograph of a latent fingerprint taken at the scene of a crime. A fourth involved a man's body washed up on an Italian beach during World War II. The army sent his prints to the FBI, which identified him from prints obtained many years earlier when he had registered as an alien in New York. A fifth was a victim of amnesia identified from prints obtained when she had applied for jobs some years earlier. A sixth involved FBI assistance in reuniting two brothers who had been separated for thirty-three years. In a seventh, a man who applied for a job as an accountant with the Atomic Energy Commission was turned down because "his fingerprint record disclosed a long police record." The eighth, and last, was a man whose right hand was found in the stomach of a shark caught at Miami Beach. The prints on the hand turned out to be those of a seaman whose tanker had been sunk off Florida.

Many of Whitehead's stories—the woman with amnesia, the long separated brothers, the body washed up on a beach in Italy, and the hand in the shark's stomach—served the bureau's interest in getting people to come forward and give their prints voluntarily to the FBI. Amnesia stories, in particular, have been popular in bureau literature. Over the years, millions of people have been persuaded to volunteer their fingerprints when they took the bureau's tour of its Washington headquarters. They were urged on by J. Edgar Hoover who said, "The time is rapidly approaching when every honest citizen will *want* his fingerprints on file. Fin-

6. This case was intended to show the FBI's concern with the rights of defendants. An FBI official is quoted by Whitehead as saying, "No matter how low a man may be, he has civil rights. So we sent the FBI's report back to the U.S. Attorney in San Francisco." Ibid., p. 137. Presumably, this episode did not require consultation of the FBI files. All it required was the equipment with which to match the prints of the narcotics peddlar against the print of the envelope.

gerprinting is liberty insurance except for those who desire to conceal the fact that they are enemies of society."

Apprehending fugitives through subsequent arrest, because they are accident victims or because they seek jobs which are checked with the FBI, does lend a certain serendipitous value to the fingerprint files. This makes the files serve a function analogous to the full searches to which police subject some motorists stopped for traffic violations. In both instances a certain number of criminals are apprehended. And both involve the happenstance of contact with the police rather than investigations centering on *modus operandi* that Clarence Kelley and other law enforcement officials like to describe.

A more systematic way to locate fugitives would be to require all citizens to be fingerprinted once a year or to have random identity checks of persons on the street. However, since most Americans would recoil from such procedures, the common practice is to check those people who, for whatever reason, come in contact with police. Some "hits" are inevitable.

Of course, some criminals are apprehended as a result of *modus operandi* investigations. Almost invariably, such investigations are conducted by a local law enforcement agency without resort to any central federal or state system of arrest records. If drugstores or supermarkets in a given section of Dallas are being robbed by people answering to similar descriptions, police may stake out likely targets of those robbers. If women in a section of Chicago are being attacked and raped by someone who ties them up with a clothesline, that will also set off an investigation based on *modus operandi*. The arrest and conviction records in the files of that police department are only infrequently of any value, and the FBI's files, organized by fingerprints, are utterly useless in such investigations.

Apprehension of a criminal, if it takes place, will result from a study of the criminal's *modus operandi* by detectives directly assigned to the case. It will not aid the Dallas police to know that Ann Arbor, Michigan, or Portland, Maine, also suffered from a series of drugstore robberies; Chicago police will not nab the clothesline rapist because they discover that somebody with the same habits previously attacked women in Tampa or Cleveland. Almost by definition, *modus operandi* is a local phenomenon. The criminal with the same style in other cities, or even in other sections of the same city, is, in all probability, a different person.

The FBI acknowledges its interest in what I believe is the real purpose served by the fingerprint files. "A person's criminal history is extremely important in assisting federal employers to make well informed decisions about whom they hire," said Clarence Kelley in his March 1974 Senate testimony. "We are also concerned with the prohibition on the use of criminal offender records for screening in certain vital and sensitive industries in the private sector, such as banking and securities. . . . Many jurisdictions require a fingerprint check before issuing licenses to purchase firearms [7] or to be a private detective, a pharmacist or an attorney. . . . The public deserves this protection and we would be remiss to deny it. Therefore we would prefer to permit a wider dissemination of criminal arrest records to non-criminal justice agencies, but with restrictions."

Maintenance and dissemination of records appears to be a larger part of the cause than of the solution for crime. To escape their dossiers, people go on the run. By moving to another place they hope to begin afresh. Attempts to escape the stigma of criminal records helped settle the West. Today, there is no frontier left to settle. Nevertheless, Americans are still on the move, more nomadic than ever before. They find it harder and harder to escape so they move with increasing frequency.

7. This writer would deny anyone the right to possess firearms, whether or not the person has a conviction record. In one stroke, that would eliminate more serious crimes than the FBI ever could.

The states with the highest crime rates in America appear to be California and Florida.[8] They are two of the five states which have been growing fastest (the other three, Alaska, Arizona, and Hawaii, also have high crime rates). According to the Bureau of the Census, between 1965 and 1970, 56 percent of the people in California and 56 percent of the people in Florida changed residences, while nationwide 47 percent of Americans changed residences. The lowest crime rates are in North Dakota, South Dakota, and West Virginia, the only states to lose population in the decade between 1960 and 1970.

Among large industrial states, the lowest crime rate seems to belong to Pennsylvania. People in that state commit crimes less than half as often as in California and Florida. Pennsylvania also has the lowest transiency rate in the country. Only 36 percent of the state's population changed addresses between 1965 and 1970.

FBI figures show Albuquerque, Miami, San Francisco, Los Angeles, and New York with the highest urban crime rates in the country. However, a study by the Law Enforcement Assistance Administration suggests that the New York crime rates are grossly overstated by comparison with other cities. The New York City

8. Because of the unreliability of crime statistics, necessarily, a hedging word like "appear" must be used. They are compiled from the data submitted to the FBI by local police departments, which vary widely in their methods for tabulating crime. For example, a city where crimes are reported by calling a central police number will not discount people known to local precincts as the neighborhood nuts. In some cities in which calls once went to precincts, major jumps in the crime rate appeared when central call numbers were first instituted. Also some police officials deliberately try to inflate or deflate the statistics for their communities to serve some purpose such as showing that they have controlled crime (which makes them deflate the figures) or showing that they need a bigger budget (which makes them inflate the figures).

Communities also vary widely in the frequency with which they report crimes to the police. If reporting the crime appears futile, as it does to residents of many communities, it is less likely to be reported.

There is nothing new or uniquely American about the manipulation of crime statistics. In the 1830s, the Russian social critic Alexander Herzen served in a provincial civil service position. His memoirs tell of the preparation of a report to the Tsar on crime: "In the draft of the provincial report appeared the statement: 'From the examination of the number and nature of crimes' (neither their number or their nature was yet known) 'Your Majesty may be graciously pleased to perceive the progress of national morality, and the increased zeal of the officials for its improvement.' " *My Past & Thoughts* (New York: Vintage, 1974), p. 255.

Police Department doesn't manipulate the figures as some other cities do, and its efficient centralized system for reporting crime insures that few complaints are disregarded. Among the cities the L.E.A.A. found to have very much higher actual crime rates than New York were Denver and Portland.

It is hard to think of Albuquerque, Denver, Portland, and Miami as particularly crime ridden. They lack the great sprawling urban ghettos of New York and Philadelphia we associate with crime. And yet, these rapidly growing sun-belt cities, attractive to the current generation of people on the run from their dossiers, have the highest crime rates in the country.

Albuquerque, which apparently ranks first in crime, multiplied in population seven times over between 1940 and 1970. Miami and Los Angeles doubled in population. Other cities with particularly high crime rates include Baton Rouge, Fort Lauderdale, Fresno, Jacksonville, Las Vegas, and Phoenix. All have been characterized by spectacular growth.

Criminologist Henry D. McKay examined trends in delinquency in seventy-four areas of Chicago under the auspices of the President's Commission on Law Enforcement. He found the greatest increase in delinquency rates in Lawndale, an area of Chicago which, in the period under study, "underwent an almost complete and very disruptive population change. A largely middle class white population was replaced by a Negro population coming partly from outside the city." At the other extreme were five areas of Chicago which had the greatest decline in delinquency. "Four out of these five areas," noted McKay, "extending in a line south from the Loop to 63rd Street, are Negro in population. This area has constituted the heart of the Negro community in Chicago for more than thirty years. . . . These areas of greatest decrease in rates of delinquency were the areas with the highest rates thirty or more years ago. At that time they resembled, in many ways, the areas of highest rates in the 1960s." [9]

9. Henry D. McKay, "A Note on Trends in Rates of Delinquency in Certain Areas in Chicago," in the Task Force Report *Juvenile Delinquency and Youth Crime*, The President's Commission on Law Enforcement and Administration of Justice, 1967, pp. 114–115.

Nineteenth-century Americans generally succeeded in leaving behind them the records of their past transgressions. They could start afresh in each new place because the machinery for disseminating their records did not exist. A chronicler of cowboy ethics (and argot) has noted, "It was a violation of code to ask a man what his name was back in the states, even if you knowed his past was full of black spots. . . . A man's past belonged to 'im alone, and should remain a closed book if he wanted it so." [10]

Hannah Arendt has attempted to explain the crimes committed by another group of people on the run, the people left stateless by the political upheavals in Europe in the 1930s. "A criminal offense becomes the best opportunity to regain some kind of human equality," she has written, because it brings them within the pale of the law, "even if it be as a recognized exception to the norm." [11] My own view is that the absence of the restraining influence of family, social institutions, and community leads nomads to crime. When these ties are severed, people will behave at their worst. In any case the connection between dislocation and crime seems so clear that the FBI's record-keeping systems, which keep people even more restlessly on the run, must be seen as a cause of crime. The very minimal investigative purposes they serve contradict the claim that they are part of the solution for crime.

10. Ramon F. Adams, *The Old-Time Cowhand* (New York: Macmillan, 1961), p. 60.

11. Hannah Arendt, *The Origins of Totalitarianism* (New York: Meridian Books, 1958), p. 286.

11

Gossip for Profit

THE CREDIT BUREAUS

Shortly after Mahlon and Leah Barash moved to Arlington, Virginia, a representative of "Welcome Neighbor" showed up to visit them. She gave them free gifts and told them about local schools and churches. In the process, the "Welcome Neighbor" hostess elicited information about the Barash family—jobs, income, expenditures, and credit cards. It wasn't until Leah Barash noticed the name Credit Bureau, Inc., on a brochure about twenty minutes after the interview started that the purpose of "Welcome Neighbor" became clear. Credit Bureau, Inc., a subsidiary of Retail Credit Company, Inc., the giant of the credit industry, with 1,500 offices around the country, has 80 local offices selling credit information to local businesses. The office in Washington, D.C., employs twenty-five "Welcome Neighbor" hostesses, whose job it is to visit newcomers like the Barash family.

According to a credit report received by the Nationwide Mutual Insurance Company, Robert Meisner and his wife earn only $5,000 a year between them. Their eighteen-year-old son, a "hippie-type youth" is "active in various anti-establishment concerns." The son, who would be driving the car, is "suspected of using marijuana on occasion." Clearly, the Meisners are not good candidates for auto insurance. And so, with that information, Nationwide canceled the Meisners' policy.

There was only one problem. The information, which had been compiled by the Retail Company, was all wrong. Robert Meisner was then an Oldsmobile salesman, and his wife is a secretary. They make a lot more than $5,000 a year. Their son is described by his principal as a "model student, a straight kid," whose "anti-establishment" activity consisted of participating in a couple of protests against the Vietnam war.

Or, take Galen Cranz, a member of the architecture faculty at Princeton University, who had her auto insurance policy canceled by State Farm Mutual Automobile Insurance Company, also on the basis of information supplied by the Retail Credit Company. In Ms. Cranz's case, the policy was canceled because Retail Credit reported that she had been living in the same house with a male friend "without the benefit of wedlock."

David Weinberger received an oral promise of a job with IBM. The job offer was withdrawn after an investigation by Retail Credit produced a report that Weinberger had been the business partner of a man indicted for mail fraud. The information was false.

The Retail Credit Company was founded in 1899. It employs 5,200 investigators or "field representatives," and, according to the company, they talk to about 150,000 people a day. That suggests about thirty conversations per day for each investigator. In "Helping Business Serve Consumers," as the slogan on its stationery puts it, Retail Credit compiles some 20 million reports on Americans a year, many of them replete with the kind of gossip that it disseminated about the Meisners and Galen Cranz. Most of the company's reports are compiled for insurance companies. Employment checks for other businesses account for about 6 million reports a year. Despite the firm's name, credit reporting for merchants accounts for only a small portion of the company's total business.

Retail Credit maintains active files on about 47 million Americans. The other large firm in the industry, TRW Credit Data, also compiles about 20 million reports a year and maintains files on about 35 million Americans. Its services are primarily drawn upon by banks, credit card firms, oil companies, small loan and sales finance companies, retailers, and other lending institutions. Unlike Retail Credit Company, TRW's files do not include gossip from neighbors, friends, and the like but are limited to information on previous credit transactions by the person about whom a report is being compiled.

The industry includes more than two thousand local credit bureaus, most of them federated by the Associated Credit Bureaus. The members of the association, which among them maintain files on about 120 million Americans, furnish about 100 million reports a year, mostly for consumer credit purposes. Such reports are sometimes comparable to those compiled by TRW and sometimes those of Retail Credit. When members of the Associated Credit Bureaus compile reports for employment checks, they are most likely to include the gossip typical of Retail Credit's files.

Retail Credit Company's rationale for its gossipy reports was explained in an interview with the company's top man in Canada, Gordon Kennedy, which appeared in the July 16, 1973, *Toronto Star*. According to the story:

If a man is "promiscuous," he [Kennedy] adds, his life expectancy may not be good. Among other risks, he could be shot by a jealous husband.

Well then—assuming insurance companies are entitled to this information—what about prospective employers? Is it fair to give them intimate details of a job-seeker's private life? "Some people wouldn't agree," Kennedy says, "but doesn't the employer have the right to make up his own mind?"

The practices of some other firms in the industry closely resemble those of Retail Credit. The Hooper Holmes firm includes such questions on its automobile insurance report form as:

Any criticism of neighborhood?
Premises poorly kept?
Personal-family reputation or associates questionable?
Any criminal record?

Hooper-Holmes's "Life-Health-Major Medical Hospitalization Report" asks:

Has he or any family member used marijuana, LSD, heroin, or other drugs as a habit?
Is he criticized for—domestic troubles, heavy debts, illegal activities, irregular beneficiary, questionable business practices?
Any criticism of his character, morals or associates?

Service Review, Inc., asks, "Do any of the following apply to this applicant: illegal or unfair business practices or dealings? Heavy debts? Domestic troubles? Arrests? Reckless driving?" O'Hanlon Reports asks, "Is his general REPUTATION as to business reliability, habits and morality at all QUESTIONABLE? (If so, explain in detail.)" For women, O'Hanlon asks, more simply, "Is her reputation in any way questionable?"

In 1973, a Senate subcommittee considered a proposal to give people about whom such reports are compiled an opportunity to find out the sources of statements that they used drugs or had bad morals or domestic troubles. The proposal encountered stiff resistance from most of the industry and was not adopted. "Hooper-Holmes strongly opposes any mandatory disclosure of sources," the company said in a statement to the Senate. "We cannot overemphasize our concern for the impact of this proposal. The mandatory disclosure of sources may well cause many, if not most, sources to become unavailable—to 'dry up.' Notwithstanding the suggestions in the testimony of other parties, it has been our experience that former employers, businessmen, bankers and other credit grantors, neighbors, and other honest and sincere people will provide factual information only so long as an express confidentiality exists. Remove the confidentiality and the sources will vanish." Hooper-Holmes did not explain how it goes about determining whether a neighbor or the subject of a report is "honest and sincere." Nor did it mention the possibility that, honesty and sincerity aside, the neighbor might be misinformed. Nor did it say why it had any business compiling information, even if it is "honest and sincere," about how well a person keeps his premises, or whether his associates are questionable, or whether a member of his family uses marijuana, or whether he has domestic troubles.

The Fair Credit Reporting Act, enacted by Congress in 1971, gives applicants for credit a limited right to know what is in the files that are kept and disseminated about them. When a person is denied credit, insurance, or employment on the basis of a credit report, the act says he is supposed to be notified of the adverse action and supplied the name and address of the credit agency. He can then contact the agency and must be told the nature of the information on which the decision was based. The credit agency is required to supply sufficient information (though not the identity of the persons who furnished the information) to allow refutation or challenge of its accuracy.

Before the passage of the Fair Credit Reporting Act, it was virtually impossible for anybody to find out if he had been hurt by an adverse credit report. Contracts between credit agencies and their customers often prohibited the customers from disclosing the source or contents of a report. The Retail Credit Company issued a manual instructing its staff what to do in the event that the person about whom a report was made called the company. "Neither deny or admit making report," the manual said. "Draw your caller out, tactfully eliciting information as to source of leak."

The Fair Credit Reporting Act is often cited as a federal law specifically intended to further the right to privacy. Between 1 and 2 percent of the people who are the subjects of credit records have used the act to find out what is in their own files. The act has not significantly reformed credit agencies' procedures for collecting, recording, and disseminating information because of the obstacles it places in the way of damage suits. The act states: "no consumer may bring any action or proceeding in the nature of defamation, invasion of privacy, or negligence with respect to the reporting of information against any consumer reporting agency, any user of information, or any person who furnishes information to a consumer reporting agency, based on information disclosed [under the FCRA] except as to false information furnished with malice or willful intent to injure such consumer."

"Malice or willful intent to injure" are virtually impossible to prove. In July 1973, more than two years after the act went into effect, according to a Federal Trade Commission official's testimony before a congressional committee, "not one dollar of damages has ever been judicially awarded to a plaintiff in a civil suit brought under the FCRA." Because it insulates credit agencies from damage suits, the act provides little incentive to credit agencies to improve the accuracy of their reporting.

Public exposure of the industry's shoddy practices is, presently, the principal inducement for credit agencies to change their ways. The Retail Credit Company was distressed by the testimony of four persons it had employed as field representatives who appeared before Senator Proxmire's Subcommittee on Consumer Credit on February 4, 1974. All four testified that they were required to produce adverse information on from 6 to 10 percent of insurance applicants. "The one who can get more adverse information can net more contracts," Richard Riley, a Retail Credit employee for fifteen years testified, because it shows that the credit agency is being more thorough than its competitors. Another former investigator, Len Holloway, described an incident in which a Miami woman had been denied automobile insurance because neighbors identified her as a "lady of the evening." Subsequently, a check with ten neighbors showed that the report was nonsense and had been based on a single interview with the "neighborhood nut." Another former investigator said reports were fabricated as a time-saving device.

While it did not respond in detail to the testimony, Retail Credit submitted a letter to Proxmire. It said the company "always has denied and continues categorically to deny" all allegations of fabricating information.

The Retail Company estimates that its reports lead to rejection of about 5 percent of credit applications. If that estimate is accurate, and if the same percentage applies to the rest of the industry, about ten million credit applications are turned down each year. (Since some people will be credit applicants more than once a year, a smaller number of people would actually be involved. At the least, using Retail Credit's figures, more than five million persons experience one or more credit rejections a year.)

The number of people actually turned down for credit may be much higher. Little of Retail Credit's business is done with small loan and finance companies. These firms, which deal with people of lower economic status than, say, credit card firms, turn down about 50 percent of loan applications, often because of credit reports. Banks, which charge lower interest rates than small loan and finance companies, and, therefore, attract people surer of their own credit standing, turn down about 10 percent of loan applications, mostly on the basis of credit reports. The smallest number of rejections occurs in the life insurance industry. The Institute for Life Insurance says that about 3 percent of applicants, or 300,000 persons a year, are turned down. Another 6 percent, or more than 600,000 persons a year, must pay extra-risk rates.

The life insurance industry maintains a specialized service for itself known as the Medical Information Bureau. MIB keeps files on the medical histories of about 12½ million Americans and shares the information with some 700 life, accident, and health insurance companies.

Most Americans believe that their medical records are private. While they submit to medical exams in order to obtain insurance policies, they do not know and are not informed that the information also goes to the Medical Information Bureau for storage in its computer and for access to any other insurance company which seeks the information. The consequences of this information sharing to Sumner Cotton, himself an insurance executive, were described in a statement by Senator Edward Kennedy before a Senate committee considering amendments to the Fair Credit Reporting Act. "Cotton," said Kennedy, "was covered by a group health policy in his company for 12 years, then he decided to go into business for himself. That meant that he had to apply for an individual health insurance policy for himself and his wife. Unfortunately, despite his contacts and knowledge of the insurance business, Mr. Cotton couldn't get a policy from anyone. It seems his wife had an episode of unexplained illness that was never diagnosed. He was told to wait several years to apply, then if she had no further problems he could get insurance. Unfortunately, she was stricken with a cerebral aneurysm a year later. Mr. Cotton's wife survived, but he is now in debt $13,000."

Kennedy proposed two reforms. First, that the medical information collected by the bureau be made available to the individual so he can challenge its accuracy and, if need be, get it corrected. Second, that an individual be allowed to prevent information about himself from going to the Medical Information Bureau. Asked by Senator Proxmire why a person's signature shouldn't be required before medical information about him was transferred to the MIB, Executive Director Joseph Wilberding responded, "The guys who wouldn't sign this are going to be the guys who are going to be crooked, and we don't think there is any quicker way to wreck a system like this than to require consent." And, when Proxmire asked about letting people see the records kept about them by the MIB, Wilberding responded, "Speaking for my organization, yes; we do object to the idea, because we think it will cost money; it won't do the individual any good; he is going to get secondary sources, whereas the real information on which he has been declined is in the hands of the company." Because the Fair Credit Reporting Act's requirements that the source of a report be disclosed to a consumer were not applied to the Medical Information Bureau, fewer than forty persons a year applied to the MIB to see their records. Most of them were not allowed to see the records.

That changed on April 1, 1974. Insurance companies affiliated with MIB began notifying insurance applicants that medical information about them would be forwarded to MIB and would be available to other insurance companies. Applicants were told the address and phone number of MIB and that they had a right to examine and challenge the information in their files. The new policy was adopted despite the hostility voiced by Wilberding, which reflected sentiment in the insurance industry. Pressure on the insurance companies from Proxmire and Kennedy was instrumental in bringing about the new policy. Its adoption did not satisfy Proxmire, who announced that he planned to press for legislation to "give a statutory base to the voluntary procedures thus far adopted."

Credit reports are used more and more for employment purposes. Retail Credit's first employment reports were compiled on applicants for jobs as insurance agents as an outgrowth of its other work for the industry. Now the company estimates that the six million or so employment reports it issues annually represent about 20 percent of all employment reporting assignments. In addition to the credit agencies, such reporting is done by specialized personnel reporting agencies, detective bureaus, and executive search organizations. A minority of employers do all their own checking. No statistics are available on the number of job applicants rejected because of such reports.

Personnel reporting got its start during the 1920s and 1930s when major industrial employers hired detective agencies to help them weed out applicants who might be likely to organize labor unions. In the 1940s, defense contractors like Lockheed Aircraft Manufacturing Corporation used such reports to help screen out saboteurs. Big companies got used to relying on credit reports on job applicants.

A leading firm in the employment servicing field, Fidelifacts, Inc., is owned and directed by former FBI agents. Vincent Gillen, president of the New York office of Fidelifacts, said in a 1968 speech to the Association of Stock Exchange Firms that his agency specialized in uncovering drinking problems, criminal records, lies on job applications, drug addiction, mental illness, and debts. If a person had heavy debts, according to Mr. Gillen, he was likely to become an embezzler; therefore, a firm like Fidelifacts regards this as important information to give to employers.

Some industries have specialized credit reporting agencies all their own. The department store industry's practices are typified by the case of Harry Brown. A sixty-year-old man with twenty-two years of retail sales experience at Macy's, Harry Brown was first hired and then quickly discharged within a two-year period by Broadstreet's, Arnold Constable, and Bonwit Teller. Brown was also turned down for advertised jobs by Wallachs, Saks Fifth Avenue, and Abraham & Strauss.

Brown's troubles started in July 1969, when he was accused by a store detective at Macy's of not promptly ringing up a sale for $6.36. He was taken to the head of Macy's security department, physically detained and questioned for two hours, and coerced into signing a confession. As soon as it was signed, Brown was fired.

After two years without being able to get a steady job, Brown was finally able to learn from Macy's that the store had reported the July 1969 incident to Stores Mutual Protective Association of New York, a credit reporting agency. None of the employers who rejected Brown for a job, or which hired him only to fire him, had advised him that they were acting on the basis of a report from Stores Mutual. Four of the incidents in which Brown had apparently been denied a job because of the damaging credit report had occurred after the Fair Credit Reporting Act went into effect on April 21, 1971. Nevertheless, none of the employers had complied with the act and advised Brown of a credit report from Stores Mutual. After he discovered the credit report, Brown applied for yet another job, this time at Bloomingdale's. Again, he was rejected. And, once again, the store never mentioned a credit report.

Harry Brown's experience is shared by many. Department stores regularly coerce confessions from suspected shoplifters and from employees suspected of pilferage or of cheating. The choice given the person taken into custody by store detectives is either sign a confession or face prosecution. The confession is sought by the store to insulate itself against a suit for false arrest. Threat of prosecution, even if the person facing it is convinced he can win acquittal, is almost always sufficient to get the statement signed.

Department stores are sometimes able to convert local police departments into credit agencies. Shortly before Christmas each year, when business is at its peak, the Louisville and Jefferson County, Kentucky, police departments circulate to stores the photographs and names of "subjects known to be active in the criminal field of shoplifting."

One person whose picture and name were circulated in this fashion was Edward Charles Davis, III, a photographer for the *Louisville Courier Journal* and *Times*. Davis had been arrested on a charge of shoplifting in June 1971. The arrest was apparently mistaken, and he was never prosecuted or convicted. The police flyer with his name and photograph on it came to the attention of Davis's employer. Davis was told that it impaired his ability to perform his job and the newspaper was considering firing him. The Kentucky Civil Liberties Union went to court on behalf of Davis to bar circulation of the flyers but lost because the judge found it significant that "dissemination of the flyers was not to the public at large but only to businessmen and merchants."

Despite the Fair Credit Reporting Act's requirement that a prospective employee turned down because of a credit report be apprised of the report, it is common for employers not to comply. Unlike the application for credit or insurance, an application for a job can be rejected for many different reasons. It is hard for the applicant to figure out that a credit report was responsible, and there is little pressure on employers to reveal the existence of such a report. This is true even though the decision to deny someone a job generally affects the person much more vitally than a decision to deny him credit, a loan, or insurance.

One state, Oklahoma, has had a law since 1910 closely regulating the credit industry. It provides that, "Whenever an opinion in writing upon the financial or credit standing of any person is about to be submitted for the purpose of establishing a financial or credit rating of customers, to be used by the retail business concerns, the person, firm or corporation submitting such opinion shall first mail a copy of such opinion to the person about whom the opinion is given at his proper post office address."

The law was enacted as part of an effort by an agrarian society to protect itself against the credit-granting Eastern establishment. Until recently, it was largely ignored. It has been rediscovered, thanks to the efforts of Paul Polin, a Tulsa businessman who has tangled in court with both Dun & Bradstreet and the Retail Credit Company. Since the statute's language limits its application to the rating of credit by credit agencies, it has not circumscribed their practices in employment screening. If it were modified to cover all the activities of credit agencies, it would be an excellent model for other states.

A growing awareness of the damage done by credit reports is producing interest in state legislatures elsewhere and in the Congress in new protective measures. Unfortunately, it is also fostering the deliberately punitive use of credit reports.

In late 1973, Alexander McFerran, director of New York City's Parking Violations Bureau, announced that the city was "tightening the screws" on scofflaws. How? By furnishing information on 250,000 people with unpaid parking tickets to credit agencies. There is no legal authority for punishment by creation of a bad credit record, but that didn't stop McFerran and others like him.

Credit bureaus have transformed gossip into a billion dollar a year business. As the law now stands, credit bureau gossip, often false, and usually irrelevant, can hurt people with virtually no possibility that the bureaus will be required to pay damages. Meaningful controls must be placed on their sometimes mischievous, often injurious operations.

12

"An FBI Agent behind Every Mailbox"
POLITICAL DOSSIERS

William Yaffe of Fall River, Massachusetts, ran for Congress in 1970. A week before election day, the local press carried a photograph of his wife Erna participating in a peace demonstration. The photograph, and a description of Erna Yaffe as a "radical activist," had been "leaked" to the press by the Fall River police.

For twenty-one months, the home telephone of Morton Halperin, an assistant to Henry Kissinger on the staff of the National Security Council for four of those months, was tapped, recording the personal conversations of Halperin, his wife, and his three children; the phone was tapped also for the seventeen months after he had left his government job; for part of that period, he was an adviser to presidential candidate Edmund Muskie. Kissinger, who read reports from the recorded conversations, says there was never any question about Halperin's loyalty.

After several hundred thousand people went to Washington, D.C., on November 15, 1969, to protest the war in Vietnam, many of them on chartered buses, paying for their trips on checks made out to the Fifth Avenue Peace Parade Committee, a principal sponsor of the rally, FBI agents visited the committee's bank to look at the names on the checks.

The method to the madness for collecting data on political

views and associations is illuminated by the experience of Lori Paton of Chester, New Jersey. She wrote a letter as part of a high school social studies assignment. Ms. Paton, who was sixteen at the time, had intended to send the letter to the tiny Socialist Labor Party, but addressed it incorrectly. As a result it went to the equally minuscule, but ideologically different, Socialist Workers Party, a Trotskyist organization, then the subject of an FBI mail cover. All mail addressed to the party was examined by the FBI, and the return addresses were recorded.

FBI Special Agent John Hugh Bryan took charge of investigating the teen-age student. "Newark indices negative re Paton," he reported. *"At Chester, N.J.* Contact sources and conduct criminal investigation regarding LORI PATON, Mile Drive, to determine if she is involved in subversive activity." The Credit Bureau in Morristown, New Jersey, had informed the bureau, a later FBI memo said, that Lori's parents, Arthur and Nancy Paton, had lived in Green Brook, New Jersey; that Arthur Paton was employed in a shop in Morristown; and before that with a Madison Avenue firm. Police Chief Edward Strait of Chester said he had no record on the Paton family; Richard Matthews, principal, and H. Werle, vice principal, of Mendham High School acknowledged that Lori Paton was a student there and was participating in a course subject on political philosophies, "From Right to Left."

The investigation turned up no discreditable information about Lori or her parents. Lori Paton's name was entered nevertheless in the index card file of the Newark FBI office. As the supervisor of the security unit of the FBI's Newark office, Special Agent Peter McDede, Jr., testified in a subsequent court proceeding, her index number describes her file as a "subversive matter."

When Lori Paton and her family learned about the FBI investigation from school officials who had been questioned by the FBI, they protested to the New Jersey ACLU. Frank Askin, a Rutgers law professor, acting for the ACLU on behalf of Lori

Paton and William Gabrielson, chairman of the social studies department of Mendham High School, wrote to J. Wallace La Prade, the FBI special agent in charge of the Newark office. Askin's letter inquiring about the investigation was answered on July 6, 1973, by Special Agent La Prade:

Dear Mr. Askin:

Your letter dated June 13, 1973, made inquiry on behalf of Ms. Lori Paton and Mr. William Gabrielson. After carefully reviewing the facts on this matter, I have concluded there was no impropriety on the part of investigative personnel of this Bureau and that the FBI has no knowledge of any letter Ms. Paton may have sent to the Socialist Labor Party. You may be assured that Ms. Paton is not the subject of an investigation by this Bureau and that the FBI does not maintain a general policy of surveillance of correspondence of political groups such as the Socialist Labor Party.

> Very truly yours,
> J. Wallace La Prade
> Special Agent in Charge

Very strictly speaking, all La Prade said was true. At the same time, the letter is a small gem of what Victor Navasky has dubbed "Hooverspeak." It is wholly and intentionally misleading.

Askin had not known that Lori Paton's letter had been misdirected to the Socialist Workers Party. This permitted La Prade to say "that the FBI has no knowledge of any letter Ms. Paton may have sent to the Socialist Labor Party." By the time Askin wrote his letter, the FBI's investigation of Ms. Paton had been completed, thus La Prade could respond in the present tense "that Ms. Paton is not the subject of an investigation." La Prade said the FBI had no "general policy of surveillance of mail to political groups like the Socialist Labor Party." He didn't mention the Socialist Workers Party, which Lori Paton had addressed by mistake, a puny party on the attorney general's list, a target of systematic FBI surveillance for at least thirty years.

Lori Paton's case set a modest legal precedent. In August 1974, a federal court ordered her FBI file destroyed. Unhappily, the court's order won't do much to deter political surveillance. No damages were awarded. And, the court declined to treat the case as a class action. Other people will have to file their own lawsuits to get their own files destroyed.

The judge refused to treat the Paton case as a class action because he worried about other "persons who may have had close affiliation with the SWP and persons who may have had illegal or suspicious activities uncovered as a result of the mail cover investigations." No principled outrage against political surveillance there. Just sympathy for one girl innocently snared in the FBI web. The denial of damages and refusal to treat the case as a class action is on appeal to a higher court.

In early 1974, an internal FBI memorandum written in 1961 by J. Edgar Hoover came to light. Headed "Socialist Workers Party Internal Security—SWP DISRUPTION PROGRAM," it said:

The Socialist Workers Party (SWP) has, over the past several years, been openly espousing its line on a local and national basis through running candidates for public office and strongly directing and/or supporting such causes as Castro's Cuba and integration problems arising in the South. The SWP has also been in frequent contact with international Trotskyite groups stopping short of open and direct contact with these groups. The youth group of the SWP has also been operating on this basis in connection with SWP policies.

Offices receiving copies of this letter are participating in the Bureau's Communist Party, USA, Counterintelligence Program. It is felt that a disruption program along similar lines could be initiated against the SWP on a very selective basis. One of the purposes of this program would be to alert the public to the fact that the SWP is not just another socialist group but follows the revolutionary principles of Marx, Lenin and Engels as interpreted by Leon Trotsky.

It is pointed out, however, that this program is not intended to be a "crash" program. Only carefully thought-out operations with the widest possible effect and benefit to the nation should be submitted. It may be desirable to expand the program after the effects have been evaluated.

Each office is, therefore, requested to carefully evaluate such a program and submit their views to the Bureau regarding initiating a SWP disruption program on a limited basis.

The nature of an FBI disruption program was spelled out in greater detail in a 1970 internal bureau memorandum outlining a series of steps to be taken against the Black Panther Party. Among the measures specified were:

Xerox copies of true documents, documents subtly incorporating false information, and entirely fabricated documents would be periodically anonymously mailed to the residence of a key Panther leader. . . . An attempt would be made to give the Panther recipient the impression the documents were stolen from police files by a disgruntled police employee sympathetic to the Panthers. . . .

A wide variety of alleged authentic police or FBI material could be carefully selected or prepared for furnishing to the Panthers. Reports, blind memoranda, LHMs [1] and other alleged police or FBI documents could be prepared pinpointing Panthers as police or FBI informants; ridiculing or discrediting Panther leaders through their ineptness or personal escapades; espousing personal philosophies and promoting factionalism among BPP members; indicating electronic coverage where none exists; outlining fictitious plans for police raids or other counteractions; revealing misuse of Panther funds; pointing out instances of political disorientation; etc. . . . Effective implementation of this proposal logically could not help but disrupt and confuse Panther activities. . . .

1. LHM stands for Letter Head Memorandum, Bureauspeak for documents on official stationery.

Quite right. Indeed it would disrupt and confuse Panther activities—and did. So much so that a high bureau official boasted to a Brandeis University political scientist studying the Justice Department that the bureau had created the feud between the Huey Newton and Eldridge Cleaver factions of the Black Panther Party. That feud destroyed the Panthers—the FBI's purpose. It also left several participants in the feud dead, which the bureau may or may not have regarded as a happy byproduct.

The FBI memos on disruption of the Socialist Workers Party and the Black Panther Party were obtained through litigation, one of two ways in which the FBI's operating methods have been disclosed. The other, more primitive, device has been theft. The theft of files from the FBI's office in Media, Pennsylvania, on March 8, 1971, produced a cornucopia of information. One of the choicest items taken by the thieves was a document on "New Left Notes—Philadelphia." The first edition of a newsletter to be "produced at irregular intervals," it proposed a plan whose chief benefit was that "it will enhance the paranoia endemic in these circles [the New Left] and will further serve to get the point across there is an FBI agent behind every mailbox." Lori Paton has learned to appreciate that point.

The idea of an "FBI agent behind every mailbox" suggests the bureau's aspirations. It is reminiscent of the two-way all-seeing television sets in 1984, or of the panopticon designed by Jeremy Bentham. The panopticon was a star-shaped prison so perfectly constructed that a single warden posted at the center of the prison could keep every inmate under perpetual surveillance. If the FBI doesn't really have the resources to put an agent behind every mailbox, the impression of omnipresence creates much the same effect. So long as the prisoners in Bentham's panopticon were aware that they were under surveillance by the warden, they were unlikely to do anything that might cause the warden any difficulty.

The FBI, born on July 1, 1908, was created by Attorney General Charles Joseph Bonaparte, a grandnephew of Napoleon I. Bonaparte took advantage of the adjournment of Congress for six months in an election year to create the bureau. Before its adjournment, Congress had refused to provide the authority for creation of any such agency. Those opposed to the establishment of the bureau argued, as did Congressman Walter Smith of Iowa, that, "No general system of spying upon and espionage of the people, such as has prevailed in Russia, in France under the Empire, and at one time in Ireland, should be allowed to grow up."

Early opponents of the bureau invoked the memory of the political police in France under the Empire in an attempt to liken the proposed Bureau of Investigation to the secret police of Joseph Fouché, who operated under Attorney General Bonaparte's ancestor, the Emperor Napoleon.

The bureau survived its bastard birth and gained legitimacy as Congress enacted laws it was intended to enforce. The Mann Act of 1910 provided its principal work in its early years. Congressional antagonism to political surveillance kept the bureau out of that line until World War I, when the Espionage Act, spy catching, and the country's preoccupation with enemy aliens conspired to overcome the inhibitions against a federal police agency concerning itself with political loyalty.

The end of the war did not end this aspect of the bureau's work. On the contrary, it increased, in part, because a rash of bombings produced a panic about radicals and aliens, reinforced by the triumph of Bolshevism in Russia.

In August 1919, the bureau established a General Intelligence Division to deal with radicals, headed by a young lawyer, J. Edgar Hoover. And deal with radicals he did—with a vengeance.

The attorney general of the United States in 1919 was A. Mitchell Palmer, himself a victim of the bombings of the period. In the Palmer raids, the attorney general, aided by the young Mr. Hoover, routed thousands of aliens and suspected radicals from their beds and arrested them without warrants. Many aliens were summarily deported.

This unhappy period in American history ended in 1924, when President Calvin Coolidge appointed Harlan Fiske Stone as attorney general of the United States. Stone stopped the bureau's loyalty investigations and ordered it to concentrate on interstate crime. Another wartime scare was responsible for the renewal of political surveillance.

On September 6, 1939, President Franklin D. Roosevelt issued the following directive:

The Attorney General has been requested by me to instruct the Federal Bureau of Investigation to take charge of espionage, sabotage, and violations of the neutrality regulations.

This task must be conducted in a comprehensive and effective manner on a national basis, and all information must be carefully sifted out and correlated in order to avoid confusion and irresponsibility.

To this end I request all police officers, sheriffs, and all other law-enforcement officers of the United States promptly to turn over to the nearest representative of the Federal Bureau of Investigation any information relative to espionage, counterespionage, sabotage, subversive activities and violations of the neutrality laws.

Inclusion of "subversive activities" in the directive was to have important consequences. The rest of the FBI's new mandate—espionage, counterespionage, sabotage, and violations of the neutrality laws—had precise relevance to the war. "Subversive activities," on the other hand, was an open-ended term. Although its context made clear that Roosevelt intended it as a target for FBI activity during the war effort, for the last thirty-five years the FBI has cited the September 6, 1939, directive as the principal legal authority for bureau political surveillance. Franklin Roosevelt's careless phrase has been employed by the bureau to justify the agent behind Lori Paton's mailbox.

The actual number of FBI agents assigned to political surveillance, of course, falls far short of the number needed to monitor every mailbox. The estimated two thousand agents with such assignments have help from thousands of undercover informers. The papers stolen from the FBI office in Media, Pennsylvania, identify as an informer a Mrs. Judy G. Feiy. She was the chief switchboard operator at Swarthmore College, and her assignment was to keep tabs on Daniel Bennett, a professor of philosophy at Swarthmore who has "been the subject of criticism by the school administration since he has taken on himself without clearing with others the responsibilities of inviting controversial speakers to the school." Mrs. Feiy was to "confidentially furnish pertinent information regarding any long distance telephone calls made or received by Bennett. She checked her slips for long distance calls made from the college for the past month and noted that none were listed as being made by Bennett."

Charles Grimm, Jr.'s assignment, which he has since admitted, was to infiltrate student groups at the University of Alabama at Tuscaloosa. In May 1970, some 150 students were arrested on criminal charges on the campus after a series of incidents of arson and violence incited by Grimm.

"Operation SAFE" (Scout Awareness for Emergency), described in the Media papers, involved twenty thousand Boy Scouts living in and near Rochester, New York. They received identification cards marked by their thumb prints. On the cards were the telephone numbers of the local police and the FBI. The Scouts participating in the program received instructions on suspicious activities. "As a result of this partnership between the Rochester, New York, Police Department and the Regional Council of the Boy Scouts," say the Media papers, "the police department has approximately 20,000 more 'good citizens' operating as extra eyes and ears for the police department." The FBI also has twenty thousand more sets of prints.

News of the activities of informers has been coming out of the woodwork with increasing frequency. Some informers have experienced pangs of conscience and have come forward. This phenomenon of self-reproach helped make J. Edgar Hoover doubtful about the White House plan for political surveillance drawn up by Tom Charles Huston. Huston proposed, among other things, stepped-up recruitment of students to spy on other students. The FBI was embarrassed by unreliable informers who were baring their souls and, also, the bureau's practices.

The FBI is not the only federal agency that is gathering data about people's political beliefs and associations. The armed services collect such files. The army's data banks include information on some 25 million Americans. This may make the army, at least quantitatively, first in the political intelligence field. The Secret Service, the House Internal Security Committee, the Civil Service Commission, the CIA, the Passport Division of the Department of State, the Customs Bureau, the Internal Revenue Service, the Office of Economic Opportunity, the Department of Health, Education and Welfare, the Post Office, and several different sections of the Justice Department all build dossiers. Most major police departments have their own "red squads" to parallel what the FBI does nationally. Private enterprise, like Agitator Detector, Inc., Wackenhut, and organizations like the right-wing Church League of America (which claims files on seven million Americans), are also active in the field. "Our files," boasts the Church League, "are the most reliable, comprehensive and complete, and second only to that of the FBI."

These days, political surveillance is on the defensive. Disclosure of the army's domestic intelligence gathering disturbed many; so did the surveillance programs disclosed by the Watergate investigations. The courts and the Congress have been slow to respond to the public distress.

By a close 5–4 margin in *Laird v. Tatum,* the Supreme Court held, in 1972, that the victims of political surveillance by the U.S. Army had no standing to seek relief in court. One who tipped the scales was William Rehnquist, who, shortly before he was appointed, had been the Nixon Administration's spokesman before Congress opposing any legal restraints on the army's political surveillance programs. Rehnquist had told the Congress that only "self-restraint" by the executive branch of government should stand against the excesses of political surveillance.

Despite the Watergate disclosures of what "self-restraint" means to the executive branch of government, there has been no congressional action to limit political surveillance.

Political surveillance limits political expression and, therefore, political change. It stifles the sense of freedom and spontaneity which should characterize democratic life. Some of its more devastating consequences have been felt by blacks, always a special target of political surveillance programs. In the Media papers was a memo from J. Edgar Hoover directing that:

Effective immediately, all BSU's [Black Student Unions] and similar organizations organized to project the demands of black students, which are not presently under investigation, are to be subjects of discreet, preliminary inquiries. . . . Open individual cases on officers and key activists in each group to determine background and if their activities warrant active investigation. Submit results of preliminary inquiries in form suitable for dissemination with recommendations regarding active investigations of organization, its leaders and key activists. . . .

This memo was followed in the Media files by another dated a few months later. It said that investigations had been "opened or reopened" on fifteen black student organizations at colleges in the Philadelphia area alone. Information that is just beginning to emerge on the surveillance and disruption programs by the FBI suggests to me that the bureau *may* have had a major role in the collapse of the black civil rights movement in the 1960s. Not enough is yet known to make categorical statements, but this is a very important question which needs to be thoroughly investigated.

The FBI's political intelligence files are consulted by the federal government and, though much less often, by state and local governments checking on job applicants. They are consulted by defense-related industries. The private firms in the political surveillance business make their money selling data to private employers.

Most private employers never check a political intelligence data bank; still, for a significant number of people, the kind of job they can get will be limited by their political dossiers.

In bad times, political dossiers can have a devastating impact. Many of the people labeled as "reds" or "pinks" by congressional committees and by such private firms as Aware, Inc., were hounded to financial ruin, and worse, during the Joseph McCarthy period. Although there seems no prospect that the country will revert to that mood any time soon, it is hardly possible to assert with confidence that the country has permanently rid itself of the strain in the national character which makes us periodically turn on people perceived to have subversive thoughts and associations.

In the summer of 1966, the House Un-American Activities Committee summoned a number of young radicals to testify, among them Abby Hoffman and Jerry Rubin, not yet nationally known figures. Rubin arrived at the hearings dressed in the costume of a Revolutionary War soldier. Hoffman was sworn in by, as the *New York Times* delicately described it, raising his right hand with his fist clenched and his middle finger erect.

Previously congressional investigations of political dissidents were attacked as "exposure for exposure's sake." The 1966 hearings were welcomed by people like Hoffman and Rubin precisely because they provided exposure for exposure's sake.

The committee, and its rotund Texas chairman, the late Joseph Pool, were baffled. Unlike the middle-class college professors, writers, directors, and actors who were the committee's chief victims in the 1940s and the 1950s, and who often stood to lose a great deal because of exposure before the committee, Hoffman and Rubin could only gain. They welcomed the hearings.

People caught up in the middle-class world of work, family, and installment payments are far more vulnerable to political repression than the students, hippies, and yippies who led the way in protesting the war in Vietnam.

Now that streakers and their successors, whoever they may be, have replaced antiwar pickets on college campuses, political leadership has again reverted to people who are vulnerable to the uses which can be made of political dossiers.

13

The Computer Is Not the Villain

Not long ago a proud new father walked into a bank to open an account in trust for the son who had been born the previous night. He filled out the appropriate forms and presented them to a bank officer, who looked them over to see if anything was missing. Indeed, something was missing, and the bank officer asked for the child's Social Security number. The father explained that it was a little early for that, and the bank officer explained that it was a prerequisite. The scene ended with the father walking out, shaking his head and muttering, "My God, he doesn't even have a name yet."

These days, a lot of people want to know your Social Security number. It goes on your tax return. Your insurance company wants it. So does your bank, and the motor vehicle license agency. In several states it is your automobile license number. The armed services now use it as the military serial number. Even your doctor wants it.

In recent years, the Congress has considered proposals which would give everyone a Social Security number at birth or on entering school. So far, such proposals have been defeated. They will be back.

The increasing use of the Social Security number suggests it will be used to link together separate data systems as a kind of universal identifier. It is a serious possibility. That does not mean that there is a sinister purpose behind every request for the Social Security number. Often it is requested by public and private agencies without any thought as to the reasons for wanting it. But while the reasons may be innocent or unthinking, the widespread use of Social Security numbers does raise the specter of computer consolidation of personal information.

Not that the Social Security number is absolutely essential for computer consolidation. It would make matters easier but, even using just names and street addresses, computers can do quite a lot.

The people who operate the computer programs have helped to focus attention on themselves by the acronyms they have chosen to identify their data banks. My own favorite acronym is SMILE—Something Meaningful In Local Effort—the Orange County, California, program which stores predelinquency records (see Chapter 3). The computer acronym scene was surveyed in the March 1974 issue of the ACLU Foundation's *Privacy Report:*

In Cincinnati the computerized file on criminals is CLEAR (County Law Enforcement Applied Regionally) and in Pennsylvania it's CLEAN (Commonwealth Law Enforcement Assistance Network). In Illinois it LEADS (Law Enforcement Agencies Data System), but in Massachusetts it LEAPS (Law Enforcement Agencies Processing System).

Selecting a name and, commonly, an acronym is an important part of establishing any kind of computer system. A name shows affection to the machine; it provides it with personality. Simple acronyms slip into common usage and overcome resistance to automation. And the acronyms tell a lot about the intent of the systems developers and users.

The Kansas City police call their system ALERT II (Automatic Law Enforcement Response Time); Connecticut has CONNECT (Connecticut On-Line Enforcement Communication and Teleprocessing); Iowa catches criminals with TRACIS (Traffic Records and Criminal Justice Information System). Lowell, Mass., has a BEAT (Breaking, Entering and Auto Theft) program.

Federal agencies are less imaginative in naming their criminal data systems: TECS (Treasury Enforcement Communications System), CADPIN (Customs Automatic Data Processing Intelligence Network), or CCH (The FBI's Computerized Criminal History file).

A futuristic sound helps: ORACLE in Los Angeles (Optimum Record Automation for Courts and Law Enforcement), Miracode in Berkeley, California, and PROMIS, in the District of Columbia U.S. Attorney's Office (Prosecution Management Information System). Some systems are named with as much pride as local landmarks: In San Francisco, it's CABLE (Computer Assisted Bay Area Law Enforcement) and in Missouri, of course, it's MULES (Missouri Uniform Law Enforcement System).

Juvenile record systems have a paternalistic tone; the acronyms convey an attempt to alter the behavior of a wayward youth. "Could anyone criticize a computer who CARES?" asks Rep. Margaret M. Heckler, R.-Mass., in reference to Computer-Assisted Regional Evaluation System, an experimental program to formulate recommendations to juvenile probation officers. Another system promises to AJJUST (Automated Juvenile Justice System Technique). AJJUST includes a Correctional Probability Aid Module that selects for a child a treatment program most likely to be successful based upon experience with similar juvenile offenders. St. Louis' system affords JURIS (Juvenile Uniform Referral Information System) and Utah's is called PROFILE.

Doctors are imaginative; the Massachusetts General Hospital Utility Multi-Programming System among medical institutions is affectionately called MUMPS. Lawyers have bright ideas, too. The University of Oklahoma retrieves legal information with a GIPSY (General Information Processing System). Ohio lawyers use an OBAR (Ohio Bar Automated Research). QUIC-LAW is, not surprisingly, a project of Queen's

College, Kingston, Ontario. Legal researchers can inquire into these systems with a KWIC—a key word in context—or with a KWOC—a key word out of context.

The great worry for citizens is the ability of all these machines to get together. If MULES gets MUMPS and GIPSY LEAPS to the ALERT and CONNECTS with CLEAN ORACLE, we are doomed.

Computerization makes consolidation of information far easier than is possible if each of the record-maintaining agencies does its work manually. It would be a mistake, however, to regard the computer as the villain of this book. The two largest and most harmful data banks examined here—the FBI's Identification Division and the Retail Credit Company—are both old-fashioned manually operated systems. They are being computerized in order to speed the process with which they furnish information. Until now information generally has been sent through the U.S. mail several days after it was requested. It will take years to complete the conversion to computers of these two giant data banks. In the interim, the FBI Identification Division will continue to operate as it has for fifty years and Retail Credit as it has for seventy-five. That is fast enough for the information to influence a personnel department trying to decide whether to hire someone.

The fragmentary information supplied without the benefits of computer consolidation is complete enough to deny someone a job. It is quite sufficient, usually, to gather in news of one major blemish: an arrest, a bad discharge from the army, enrollment in a drug maintenance program. Much of this information is discovered simply from employment application forms. The data bank is then used to check on the truthfulness of information provided by the job applicant.

The FBI also operates the fully computerized National Crime Information Center. NCIC stores and disseminates far less data, the recipients of the data are fewer and more highly selected, the purposes are more rigidly limited. NCIC has drawn far more fire than the Identification Division from Congress, the press, and the public just because it is computerized.

As a consequence of the preoccupation with computers, the FBI has been able to obscure its handling of data. Every so often, the bureau issues a statement describing some new privacy safeguard that has been introduced into the NCIC. What the bureau fails to say is that the giant, but slow, manual Identification Division continues along disseminating data as promiscuously as ever.

The concern about computers was stimulated by several of the books about privacy published in the 1960s. The best of those books, *Privacy and Freedom* by Alan F. Westin, made a strong case that computerization would inevitably result in data sharing and would destroy practical limits on privacy. When Westin returned to the subject a few years later in a study for the National Academy of Sciences, examining the data banks maintained by fifty-five public and private agencies, this earlier prediction was recanted.[1] "Our basic finding is quite strong. The organizations that we visited have not extended the scope of their information collection about individuals as a direct result of computerization." Westin and Baker found "that the information that is considered most sensitive and subjective in each type of organization has not yet been put into the computerized files, but is being maintained in manual records."[2] In the credit industry it is a lot easier to computerize the relatively objective data about previous credit transactions compiled by TRW Credit Data than the gossip supplied by Retail Credit. It would require fairly elaborate computer coding to accept, say, a neighbor's comment that a woman is a "lady of the evening."

The purposes of most data collection programs are fairly humdrum. Those who gather the information are not interested in

1. *Databanks in a Free Society*, written in association with Michael A. Baker (New York: Quadrangle, 1972).
2. Ibid., p. 249.

a person's whole life. They are in search of fragments of information that will help them put people into slots. An episode will decide whether a child is put in one class or another, whether a young man should be permitted to enlist in the navy, whether he should be given a job, get credit, or be allowed to rent an apartment. Once a salient fact enters the record—the army says he is a homosexual, the police say he was arrested, the credit bureau says he is irresponsible—it closes off further inquiry. The department store personnel officer won't hire a job applicant who is in a drug maintenance program because, if the person should steal something, the store detectives will blame the person who did the hiring. An employment agency will not refer a person with an arrest record for a job because the employer won't send any more business to that agency. The hack bureau won't license a former mental patient to be a cab driver because of the bad publicity if he should be involved in a fatal accident.

Taken separately, each of those judgments seems quite rational. Taken together, judgments based on such fragmentary information produce grave social consequences. It may be statistically true that a person enrolled in a drug maintenance program is more likely to steal from a department store than some other job applicant. The person rejected because he is in a drug program might not, in fact, steal anything, and the person chosen might walk away with half the store. But the record suggests a statistical probability which is hard to ignore. A computer printout which told the personnel officer the whole life story of the job applicant in a drug program would not change the decision to deny that person a job. It would simply be surplus information. Westin and Baker's finding that computerization has "not extended the scope of [the] information collection about individuals" doesn't reflect any special concern about individual rights by the data bank managers. Quite enough information was being collected before computerization to make it unnecessary for them to add more.

And quite enough information is collected by some of the manual systems still in operation. If they computerize it is because it is economic to do so and not because of a master plan to consolidate data banks.

The computerization and consolidation of personal data would raise a problem this book does not assess. This is the possibility that a would-be totalitarian government would use integrated knowledge of us to secure total power over us.

During an appearance before the U.S. Senate Subcommittee on Consumer Credit, Senator William Proxmire asked the executive director of the Medical Information Bureau whether his organization's computer files on the medical histories of 12½ million Americans included information on psychiatric treatment. The answer was yes. Proxmire commented that the White House "plumbers" might have saved themselves the trouble of burglarizing the office of Daniel Ellsberg's psychiatrist and simply consulted the MIB data bank. Proxmire's comment, shrugged off by the man from MIB, does suggest the dangers inherent in computerized data banks capable of ready exchange of information with each other. The people who set the "plumbers" their task also came up with an "enemies" list. It would have been terribly convenient for them in their efforts to harass and embarrass the "enemies" if they could have gone to a central computer, fed in identifying codes (such as Social Security numbers) on each of the persons on the list, and requested a printout on each "enemy."

The possibility that this scenario may someday be real justifies Luddite sentiments. The data banks can be transformed into efficient social control instruments of a totalitarian society.

But contemporary America is not a totalitarian society. The "plumbers" and "enemies" phenomena were kept secret by the Nixon Administration because it feared the political consequences. And indeed, once the public learned of those enterprises, it demanded punishment of the officials responsible.

Helping business serve business is the purpose of most data collection, even if it is not "Helping Business Serve Consumers," as claimed by Retail Credit. I think data collection does a great disservice to both the real and the avowed purposes by labeling millions of Americans as pariahs. But the computer is not the culprit. The problem is not getting worse as technologically advanced systems replace manual operations. It could hardly get worse.

14

On the Costs and Benefits of Lying

Writing about Stalin's purges, Nadezhda Mandelstam and Alexander Solzhenitsyn observed that victims who deemed themselves to be innocent nevertheless believed their fellow sufferers to be guilty. Because they thought of others as true criminals, they were unable to join their fellow victims in action to protect themselves.

Few self-help movements have emerged in the United States among people victimized by their records. Those who have been arrested but not convicted often think their own cases are exceptional but share in the general presumption that other people with similar records were guilty. So many are tarnished by a record of arrest that among them must be a number of those who, in turn, make the decisions to deny jobs to other people who have similar records. Common experience has proven no guarantee of empathy.

The failure to organize self-help movements runs counter to the American experience. "Americans of all ages, all conditions, and all dispositions, constantly form associations," said de Tocqueville. Not all conditions and dispositions. Many of the groups stigmatized by their records have not organized. Each individual hopes to escape his record by concealing it.

Of the numerous stigmas records impose, the most difficult to conceal are criminal convictions; yet, it is the exconvicts who, among all groups described in this book, have organized best in their own behalf. There are hundreds of organizations of exconvicts; they publish newspapers, present testimony at legislative hearings, give speeches to civic organizations, and help other exconvicts get jobs and homes. Many public and private social work agencies concentrate on securing a "second chance" for exoffenders. The very difficulty of concealing conviction records apparently makes exconvicts face up to the problem.

By contrast, no one speaks for those with arrest-but-no-conviction records. No one will help them get jobs. Their cause should be far more eligible for public sympathy since they must be assumed innocent. Those with arrest records prefer not to identify themselves or join with others whom they think were probably guilty. Getting by without disclosing the record seems to them the best option.

Erving Goffman has noted that, "The stigmatized individual exhibits a tendency to stratify his 'own' according to the degree to which their stigma is apparent and obtrusive. . . . [T]he hard of hearing" says Goffman "stoutly see themselves as anything but deaf persons, and those with defective vision, anything but blind. It is in his affiliation with, or separation from, his more evidently stigmatized fellows that the individual's oscillation of identification is most sharply marked." [1]

Individuals with arrest records are like the hard of hearing and those with defective vision. They try to separate themselves from those with the greater stigma of a conviction, who are like the deaf and the blind. This makes it difficult to act in their own behalf.

Some people trying to escape their past records deliberately plot how they will conceal them. Goffman observed that mental patients in St. Elizabeth's Hospital in Washington, D.C., would

1. Erving Goffman, *Stigma* (Englewood Cliffs, N.J.: Prentice-Hall, 1963), p. 107.

discuss strategy for passing as persons without records after they got out.

For the first job, official entree would necessitate the employer knowing about their stigma, and perhaps the personnel officer, but always the lower levels of the organization and workmates could be kept in some ignorance. Patients expressed the feeling that after staying in a placement job of this kind for six months, long enough to save money and get loose from hospital agencies, they would quit work and, on the basis of the six-month record, get a job someplace else, this time trusting that everyone at work could be kept ignorant of the stay in the mental hospital.[2]

A similar strategy was used in the eighteenth century by Daniel Defoe's heroine, Moll Flanders. Moll's adventures included burglary, bigamy, incest, and prostitution. She is transported to Virginia as a felon along with one of her husbands. It is important to her to settle near people living alongside of the Potomac River, but she fears identification as a criminal and warns her husband of "the absolute necessity of our not settling in Potomac River, that we should presently be made public there." Moll and her husband settle a few hundred miles away, build new identities for themselves, and after a year return to the Potomac, "sure of agreeable reception, and without any possibility of a discovery of our circumstances."

In recent years, stigmatized groups such as welfare recipients and homosexuals have organized in their own behalf. There is even a nascent movement of ex–mental patients. Only a tiny fraction of these people have identified themselves with such movements. At its height, the National Welfare Rights Organization claimed a membership of 100,000, a fraction of 1 percent of the country's welfare recipient population. The gay liberation

2. Ibid., p. 94.

groups, whose efforts attract public attention, have been successful in reducing discrimination against homosexuals; only a tiny fraction of the people for whose interests they speak participate. Organizations of ex–mental patients are, relatively, tinier still.

All of these self-help organizations, like less stigmatized groups—women, American Indians, servicemen, and so on—learned from the example of the black civil rights movement. Equally influencing their recent emergence is their knowledge that they now have no hope of escaping their stigmas by passing. The dissemination of dossiers has become too efficient.

Each year, thousands of homosexuals in California are convicted of public lewdness, often when a policeman in a homosexual cruising area, and dressed in what appears to be homosexual garb, has encouraged someone to solicit. California law requires that records of convictions for public lewdness be reported to certain employers. The dissemination of those records to employers has confronted many homosexuals with the impossibility of staying in the closet. Once forced to accept the visibility of their stigma, they organized gay activist groups, now as strong in California as anywhere in the country.

People stigmatized by their records without knowing it, of course, are the least likely of all to organize in their own behalf. These include high school students labeled as troublemakers by records they never see and veterans with honorable discharges burdened by unfavorable code numbers whose meanings they do not know. To them, lying or passing is irrelevant. They don't know enough about their records to lie about them. But what they don't know still hurts them.

Of course, not all employers inquire about records. They are not a significant factor in the hiring of farm labor or for jobs in many small manufacturing plants or service industries. If an applicant for a job as a dishwasher, messenger, cleaner and presser, or gas station attendant is asked about his record, the inquiry generally stops there. In many communities, no one checks further with the local police department or credit bureau.

A candidate for a low-paying job in a relatively marginal industry can often get away with lying about his past record. Other jobs will be beyond his reach because the lie will be discovered. It will probably be found out if he seeks public employment, or a job with a major private employer such as a large manufacturing firm or a department store. Any job which requires a special license—from cab driver to physician—will probably result in exposure of the lie.

Some public jobs are available to people with bad records. A Georgetown University Law Center study[3] found significant numbers of people with arrest and conviction records employed in unskilled jobs by public agencies. The study also found, however, that people with records screen themselves out. They

initiate applications for employment but do not complete them when they see questions about previous arrests or convictions. . . . Furthermore, the reputation an agency receives by asking such questions may be transmitted by word of mouth, thus other persons may not even bother to start the application process, knowing in advance what they will find. Interviews with several officials of minority self-help programs substantiated this problem, in part because they gave this advice themselves.

George Carter lied his way into a job. He is a tall, handsome, prosperous-looking black man in his late thirties, is married, has two children, a good job, lives in the suburbs, and meets his mortgage payments. Altogether, he is the sort of solid citizen whose liberal neighbors are happy to have him integrate their corner of Westchester.

Carter (not his real name) came to see me because he had a

3. Herbert S. Miller, *The Closed Door*, 1972.

problem. He was being promoted. He thought it would tear his world apart.

Almost twenty years earlier, when he was nineteen, Carter was arrested and convicted of armed robbery. He and two friends had held up a gas station. Because it was a first offense for Carter, he got a relatively light sentence. After two years, he was out of prison.

Carter never went back to his home town. Instead, he moved to a nearby college community, which was home for a friend he met in prison. For a while, he lived with his friend's aunt and worked as a grocery-store delivery boy.

In his spare time, Carter began hanging around the college campus, and in particular, the chemistry laboratories. If there was work to be done, he would pitch in to help. He became familiar with the laboratory routines, and when a job as a laboratory assistant became available, he was hired to fill it.

Carter worked at the laboratory for four years. He began to take courses at the college, though he never enrolled as a student; that didn't seem to him possible since he had been a high school dropout. He did manage to pick up such outward appearances of a college education as the appropriate speech patterns.

When the professor who hired Carter to work in the laboratory moved to another college, Carter decided to move. He went to New York and, after a couple of false starts, got a job in a firm manufacturing laboratory paraphernalia. From there, Carter moved to a television network, which was on the lookout for black employees to help it meet the rising demand for integration of production crews.

By the time Carter visited me, he had been employed by the network for seven years. He was a producer in charge of his own crew and was being promoted to be put in charge of a traveling crew. In that job, he would have a large amount of cash to spend as needed on location and, therefore, would have to be bonded.

Carter came in to see me with the bond company's application form in his hand. It asked about arrests and convictions. It also asked about education. He had told the network when he was hired that he had attended college, which was true in a way, though he had never been enrolled. He had also said that he had never been arrested, which was a lie.

Should he lie again? Should he quit and get another job? He didn't think he could revert to his old job and just forget about the promotion. He had worked too hard for it, and everybody knew he wanted it.

Carter's story has a happy ending. I told him that the bonding company would probably find out about his armed robbery conviction and might discover his lack of a college education. Lying again would hurt him more than anything else. His best bet was to go to the highest official he knew at the company and tell the whole story. Being black might even help him.

Two weeks later, Carter called me and told me he had made a clean breast of it, and it had worked. He was even going to get bonded and would have his promotion.

It would be nice to conclude this brief account of George Carter with the moral that honesty is the best policy. Unfortunately, it wouldn't be true. If Carter had told the truth about his conviction for armed robbery, he never would have been hired in the first instance by the television network. After seven years of faithful and reliable service, the company was willing to accept the notion that what a man did twenty years earlier doesn't necessarily determine the way he will act in wholly different circumstances. Carter got the chance for those seven years of service by lying.

Carter's progression from the small company manufacturing laboratory equipment to the television network is the time-honored way to lie one's way into a really good job. By working satisfactorily for a firm which did not check his background, Carter established a past for himself which the television network could examine before hiring him. Fortunately for him, that is the only checking that was done.

Norman Amsterdam wasn't so lucky. Amsterdam (not his real

name) ran away from home at fourteen. For the next few years he was on the run. Along the way, he was arrested and convicted for several minor offenses. At twenty-two, in Denver, he was married to a girl also on the run, but with no record. She got a job for a poverty agency, and he was a gas station attendant. For five years, they saved almost every penny they earned; then he applied to an oil company to buy a franchise for a gas station of his own. Amsterdam's juvenile record turned up even though he had concealed it; the franchise application was rejected.

I am not asking readers to suspend moral judgments about the lies told and lived by George Carter and Norman Amsterdam and many others like them. Especially in the wake of Watergate, I shrink from the suggestion that there is a higher good that is served which makes it all right to lie. But there are benefits which George Carter *and the rest of us* derive from such lies. In acquiring a responsible job, a home, and a family, Carter made himself a different person from the youngster with the same name who held up the gas station. It was in his own interest to effect this transformation. But it was also in the interest of the gas station owner or grocer who might otherwise have become Carter's next victim. Carter's successful lie was the critical ingredient in the remaking of his life. I can't help wishing Norman Amsterdam had similarly succeeded. If more people could get away with such lies, we would have fewer muggings and burglaries to fear.

A lot of things have been tried in an effort to reduce criminal recidivism. We have put people in prison for long and short periods. We have varied the conditions of prison, parole, and probation. There is no evidence that any of these approaches has any significant impact on recidivism. Prison and parole do not rehabilitate. At least 65 percent of those people once convicted of crime will again be convicted. A good many of the remaining 35 percent will also commit crimes and just won't get caught.

The only sure cures for recidivism are capital punishment or life imprisonment without parole. Those who favor such penalties would generally limit them to murderers, among all criminals the least likely to be recidivists. We are not bloodthirsty enough to execute millions of burglars. Keeping them all in prison for life would be repugnant because of its financial cost, as well as for other reasons.

But while we are too humane to impose extreme punishment, we resist the small steps needed to integrate criminals into our social and economic mainstream and, thereby, mitigate their danger to our peace of mind and our safety. When someone gets away with a lie about an arrest, a conviction, or some other aspect of his past, he may rehabilitate himself. That's what George Carter did.

15

Race and Records

For most of the last thirty years, unemployment among blacks has been about twice as frequent as among whites. It was exactly double in 1972 when, according to the Bureau of Labor Statistics, black unemployment averaged 10 percent and white unemployment averaged 5 percent.

It wasn't always that way. The 1930 census, taken before the Depression was in full swing, showed black unemployment nationwide at 6.1 percent, actually lower than the white rate of 6.6 percent. At the time most blacks still lived and worked in the rural South. Even outside the South, blacks were only unemployed about half again as often as whites in 1930. The disparity between unemployment rates which we almost take for granted today developed within the last forty years.

The Depression years and the war years set in motion a great migration of blacks from the rural South to the North. Industrial jobs were the lure. And while few jobs were available in the North during the Depression, those that did exist paid a survival wage. The migration North was spurred by a romantic view of life. As one blues couplet had it:

> Michigan water taste like sherry wine,
> Mississippi water, taste like turpentine.

Every so often a "Black Ulysses" would return to his home in the rural South and tell of the marvelous adventures encountered in his travels, but life wasn't really so pleasant for the migrants. "The solitary wandering men and women are in the majority of cases the debris," wrote black sociologist E. Franklin Frazier. They are "thrown off by a bankrupt and semi-feudal agriculture in the South.... These men and women have not only been up-rooted from the soil but have no roots in a communal life and have broken all social ties. Their mobility has emancipated them in many cases from the most elementary forms of social control." [1]

Mass migration from farm to city has often produced severe social problems. The dislocation of many thousands of people in England in the late sixteenth century and early seventeenth century by enclosure of the fields made London a refuge for ragtag armies of vagabonds and beggars. They created a crime problem in seventeenth-century London of far more fearsome proportions than is known to any contemporary American city.

As a resident of New York City, I periodically am titillated by comparisons of present-day crime rates between my city and London. The infrequency of crime in London makes that city seem almost too good to be true. In the last three centuries, the descendants of the seventeenth-century cutthroats have become a very peaceful lot. By contrast, New York houses great numbers who have not yet put down roots. The situation is even worse in the rapidly growing sun-belt cities from Florida to Oregon which are presently favored by the nomads crisscrossing these United States.

While migrants get into trouble much more than other people, after a time they put down roots. The passage of time reduces the disparity between them and everybody else. At least, that is the way it used to be. It has even been that way for some blacks moving to cities. At the beginning of this century, there was a movement of blacks from the rural South to southern cities like

1. *The Negro Family in the United States*, rev. ed. (Chicago: University of Chicago Press, 1966), p. 224. Originally published in 1939.

Atlanta. That city's blacks have put down roots. Atlanta today has the best educated, most prosperous, and most politically powerful black community in the country. Its reputation is building a "reverse migration" in which blacks are returning to the South from other parts of the country.

The advent of big-time record keeping has changed what happens to migrants. Now, people who get into trouble are quickly labeled as troublemakers and, thereby, excluded from jobs, schools, the armed services, and other social institutions. In the process the label of troublemaker becomes self-reinforcing.

Unfortunately, the great migration of blacks from the rural South to the North coincided with the development of dossier building. The FBI's Identification Division was established in 1924. In the late 1920s school records began including "whole-child" information instead of grades alone. The social welfare legislation of the New Deal in the 1930s included many provisions for the maintenance and dissemination of records. The Selective Service System was established in 1940.

All of the stigmatizing record-keeping systems discussed in this book label blacks in greatly disproportionate numbers, and by about the same ratios. Blacks get bad discharges from the armed forces about 2½ times as often as whites; get arrested about 2½ times as often as whites; and get convicted about 2½ times as often as whites.

In the minds of many people, crime and blacks are virtually synonymous. And, indeed, while blacks made up only 11.1 percent of the population, according to the 1970 census, according to the FBI crime reports for 1971, blacks accounted for 27 percent of all arrests. In rural areas blacks accounted for 10.8 percent of the population and 10.3 percent of all arrests. The disproportionate frequency with which blacks get arrested is an urban phenomenon.

It is part of the liberal dogma of our time that poverty breeds crime, yet, blacks, like Chicanos, in rural areas are, if anything, poorer than their city cousins. Moreover, rural blacks today are well aware of the relative wealth of other people; the television set now reaches into virtually every poor rural hovel. Perhaps the most impoverished area in the country is the lower Rio Grande Valley of Texas, home base for hundreds of thousands of Chicano migrant workers who live in rural slums without even clean drinking water, but with television sets and even cable hookups to receive Spanish-language programs from Mexico City.

Even greater disparities than between white and black exist in the labeling of males and females. About four times as many males will acquire arrest records as females. About four times as many *black* males will acquire arrest records as *black* females. The ratio of convictions between males and females is also about four to one. Selective Service records never label females, and military discharges almost never stigmatize females.

More than anyone in our society, urban black males are labeled unfit by their records. The staggering statistic that 90 percent of them can expect to be arrested at some point in their lives only begins to tell the story.

A decade ago, Daniel Patrick Moynihan caused a sensation with the publication of a report he prepared for the United States Department of Labor on "The Negro Family." It attempted to explain the reasons for unemployment and other social ills among blacks. According to Moynihan, Negro society was dividing sharply between a stable middle class, which was growing more successful, and "an increasingly disorganized and disadvantaged lower class group." By lumping these two groups together for statistical purposes, the illusion appeared that Negroes were making general economic progress. However, argued Moynihan, the condition of the understratum of Negro society was actually deteriorating. The basic cause, he said, was the disintegration of the Negro family. For lack of a cohesive family life, Negro children were started on the road to failure: they dropped out of school, were arrested as delinquents, were rejected as unfit by the army, themselves became the parents of illegitimate children, and created unstable families of their own. The pathology, therefore, could be expected to perpetuate itself.

Moynihan's thesis was not new. It owed a lot to the much earlier writings of E. Franklin Frazier and to the work of black psychologist Kenneth B. Clark, whose book, *Dark Ghetto,* was published the previous year. Nevertheless, the report was sharply attacked by some civil rights spokesmen. Floyd McKissick, then head of C.O.R.E., said that "it assumes that middle class values are the correct ones for everyone in America." Bayard Rustin said, "the report accentuated or exaggerated the negative." But by far the most frequent and important criticism was from civil rights leaders and sociologists who said that Moynihan's blaming of the Negro's troubles on the disintegration of the Negro family, as Frazier and Clark did not, was a prescription for evading government responsibility for antidiscrimination measures. These attacks came with some urgency because Moynihan's report had formed the basis of the first major address on civil rights by Lyndon Johnson during his presidency.

Moynihan's analysis of the condition of the Negro family was based on statistics which showed that almost one-fourth of all Negro families were headed by females. The males were not around as a result of divorce, separation, desertion, or other absence. The percentage of nonwhite families headed by females was more than double that of white families. Moreover, the percentage was rising in nonwhite families and declining in white families.

Male absenteeism, said Moynihan, was contributing to the emergence of a matriarchal society among American Negroes. Women played the dominant role because "segregation and the submissiveness it exacts, is surely more destructive to the male than to the female personality. Keeping the Negro 'in his place' can be translated as keeping the Negro male in his place: the female was not a threat to anyone. . . . The 'sassy nigger' [male, that is] was lynched." [2]

Even in the job market, Negro women were more successful than Negro men. In 25 percent of Negro families where the husband was present and working, the wife was still the principal earner. Among whites, the figure was 18 percent. Negro males then accounted for only 1.2 percent of all males in white collar jobs; Negro females represented 3.1 percent of the total female white collar work force. Negro males accounted for 1.1 percent of all male professionals; Negro females, 6 percent of all female professionals. Negro males accounted for 2.1 percent of all male technicians; Negro females represented 10 percent of all female technicians.

The report was, of course, written before the emergence of the contemporary feminist movement, but, Moynihan anticipated the feminist response. "There is, presumably, no special reason why a society in which males are dominant in family relationships is to be preferred to a matriarchal arrangement," he wrote. "However, it is clearly a disadvantage for a minority group to be operating on one principle, while the great majority of the population, and the one with the most advantages to begin with, is operating on another."

The women's rights movement, which aims to eliminate sex-role stereotypes, may someday mitigate the psychological tensions of matriarchal black families. If the wife is the principal wage earner, it may lead to less recrimination against the black husband than has often characterized such family relationships. Feminist ideology has not yet substantially penetrated the black community. The female-dominated black family is out of step with white society as portrayed, for example, on television.

All this, Moynihan explained by saying that slavery and

2. The report is reprinted in Lee Rainwater and William L. Yancey, *The Moynihan Report and the Politics of Controversy* (Cambridge, Mass.: MIT Press, 1967), 493 pp.

segregation were harder on the male than the female. Others have attributed the disruption of black family life to slavery's disruption of slave families. That contention has been debunked by Robert William Fogel and Stanley L. Engerman in their important study of the economics of slavery, *Time on the Cross.* They demonstrate that, "The family was the basic unit of social organization under slavery. It was to the economic interest of planters to encourage the stability of slave families and most of them did so. Most slave sales were either of whole families or of individuals who were at an age when it would have been normal for them to have left the family." [3]

If the thesis is right that male absenteeism from the Negro family is a legacy of the emasculating effects of slavery and segregation or of the break-up of families by slave sales, presumably the problem would diminish as the experience it reflects fades into history. Instead, disintegration of the black family emerged as a problem only with migration from the rural South in this century.

I contend that black male absenteeism from the home is far more a product of unemployment caused, in turn, by arrest, conviction, draft, and military discharge records—contemporary rather than historical emasculation. Leaving one community for another is a rational response to the inability to find a job near home. A bad record may not follow the person who has fled his home for another town.

Many unemployed blacks are virtually unemployable. That may be a consequence of records. If they were kicked out of school and labeled as delinquents early in life, they could not acquire the skills to qualify for most jobs. The fastest growing occupations are in professional and licensed technical fields. People with stigmatizing records have little chance there either. They are qualified primarily for manual jobs, and there aren't enough of them to go around.

3. (Boston: Little, Brown and Co., 1974), p. 5.

Moynihan concluded his report by calling for "a national effort . . . directed towards the question of family structure. The object should be to strengthen the Negro family so as to enable it to raise and support its members as do other families." If that were not done, he warned, things would only get worse. "Three centuries of injustice have brought about deep-seated structural distortions in the life of the Negro-American. At this point, the present tangle of pathology is capable of perpetuating itself without assistance from the white world. The cycle can be broken only if these distortions are set right."

In the intervening decade, the distortions have not been set right. The cycle has not been broken. The tangle of pathology has perpetuated itself. Public policy has not sought to rebuild Negro family life. On the contrary, national welfare policy often makes it economically advantageous for males to desert their families. By 1972, 32 percent of black families were without husbands, close to four times the rate among whites.

The laws governing the payment of Aid to Dependent Children (ADC) in many states require that a child be deprived of the support of at least one parent. The parent must be either dead, physically or mentally incapacitated, or away from home. For many black fathers, leaving home is the best way to insure welfare payments for their families.

Until recently, the law also discouraged a woman from engaging in a relationship with a male who would become a "substitute father." Welfare departments would cut off ADC payments when a mother had frequent visits from a male. Designed to punish the "immorality" of sexual relations between welfare mothers and their male friends, "substitute father" regulations also denied children relationships with males who could act in a fatherly way to them. These regulations were struck down by the United States Supreme Court in a 1968 case, *King v. Smith*. Many welfare departments continued to enforce such regulation nevertheless. As a result, among the white poor, only 44 percent of children had both parents in the home in 1970, and among the black poor, only 24 percent. Among all white children, 91 percent lived with both father and mother.

The Moynihan report offered no agenda for action to remedy the conditions of Negro family life. And Lyndon Johnson's civil rights speech based on the Moynihan Report, delivered at Howard University on June 4, 1965, dealt with action only in the vaguest generalities. Johnson repeated some of Moynihan's observations on the Negro family and said:

There is no single easy answer to all of these problems.

Jobs are part of the answer. They bring the income which permits a man to provide for his family.

Decent homes in decent surroundings, and a chance to learn—an equal chance to learn—are part of the answer.

Welfare and social programs better designed to hold families together are part of the answer.

Care of the sick is part of the answer.

An understanding heart by all Americans is also a large part of the answer.

To all these fronts—and a dozen more—I will dedicate the expanding efforts of the Johnson Administration.

I believe Moynihan was right in calling for the recognition of family cohesion as an important goal of public policy. Unfortunately, his psychohistorical analysis of the roots of the problem defeated any effort to deal with it. There is not a great deal any contemporary government can do to mend the psychological damage done by slavery. Moynihan made the problem seem irremediable.

A similar analysis appears in Christopher Jencks's *Inequality*.[4] He also talks in generalities about governmental action to deal with

4. (New York: Basic Books, 1972).

racial equality, and in the final sentences of his book calls for "socialism. Anything less will end in the same disappointment as the reform of the 1960s." Along the way, however, Jencks disputes the ability of public policy to bring about equality, and particularly not through the schools. Jencks finds heredity a much more important influence on learning than the schools, and family environment much more important than heredity. With Moynihan, Jencks sees the situation of the black family as a cause, rather than a symptom.

If, as I contend, stigmatizing dossiers are a major cause of the disintegration of the black family, then it is a problem amenable to government action. The problem will not be solved in the short run. That almost never happens, though if their records were wiped clean, many black males could get jobs fairly quickly. Certainly, over a period of years, the stigmas could be wiped out.

"The most certain thing about modern poverty," John Kenneth Galbraith has written, "is that it is not efficiently remedied by a general and tolerable well-distributed advance in income. Case poverty is not remedied because the specific individual inadequacy precludes employment and participation in the general advance." [5] The dossier which stigmatizes a black male is such a "specific individual inadequacy," it sends young black males on the run from the police, the armed forces, and the records which label them as "unfit" or "criminal." In the process, they run from their families as well, leaving behind the women to manage as best they can and the children to grow up without fathers.

To escape the dossiers, they have no choice but to run, as in the dream of Ralph Ellison's *Invisible Man*, who finds an engraved document with a short message from his grandfather: "To Whom It May Concern—Keep This Nigger-Boy Running."

5. *The Affluent Society* (Boston: Houghton Mifflin, 1958), p. 327.

16

Remedy

As every man goes through life he fills in a number of forms
for the record, each containing a number of questions. . . .
There are thus hundreds of little threads radiating from
every man, millions of threads in all. If these threads were
suddenly to become visible, the whole sky would look like a
spider's web, and if they materialized as rubber, trams,
buses, trains and even people would all lose the ability to
move, and the wind would be unable to carry torn-up
newspapers or autumn leaves along the streets of the city.
They are not visible, they are not material, but every man is
constantly aware of their existence.

—Alexander Solzhenitsyn
Cancer Ward

The main protection for privacy in the United States Constitution is the Fourth Amendment. It asserts "the right of the
people to be secure in their persons, houses, papers, and effects,
against unreasonable searches and seizures. . . ." The authors of
that guarantee remembered the "writs of assistance," general
warrants authorizing wide searches. Armed with such writs, British crown officers burst into the homes and mercantile offices of
the citizens of Massachusetts, arrested the occupants, seized property in lieu of the payment of taxes and destroyed much of the
remaining property. James Otis, assisted by the young John
Adams, fed the fires of revolution in Boston with eloquent

arguments that the Act of Parliament in 1699, purportedly authorizing the writs, was "an act against natural equity" and, therefore, "void. If an act of Parliament should be passed in the very words of this petition for writs of assistance, it would be void. . . ."

Today, the Fourth Amendment is most often invoked to regulate contacts between the police and citizens on the streets, in their cars and in their homes. It is the provision of the Constitution most directly in controversy in debates over "law and order." In 1961, a decision by the Supreme Court, *Mapp v. Ohio,* made it applicable to the states. Evidence seized illegally was no longer admissible in state court criminal proceedings. For a very brief period, the *Mapp* decision played havoc with the traditional methods of local law enforcement officials accustomed to searching people at will and prosecuting them on the basis of any contraband or evidence discovered. However, with a small exercise of ingenuity, police departments soon returned to their old ways. State legislatures cooperated by enacting "stop and frisk" laws, "no knock" laws, and other devices to legalize random and intrusive searches. And, most important of all, police discovered that a little perjury would provide judges with what they needed to declare any evidence seized legally admissible. "As I approached the defendant, he became apprehensive and I saw him reach into his back pocket and drop something into the gutter," the officer testifies. This allows a prosecution for possession of drugs or gambling paraphernalia without any mention of a search. In the criminal courts, these are known as "dropsy" cases, after the peculiar malady of dropping things which began to afflict criminal defendants all across the country as soon as police recovered from the shock of *Mapp.* If evidence is seized from a person's home or car, the officer now testifies the search was based on "a tip from a confidential informant whose identity cannot be revealed but who has previously provided reliable information."

The Warren Supreme Court, author of the *Mapp* decision,

started the process of eroding it by accepting some of these circumventions. The Burger Court has continued and greatly accelerated the process. As a result, there is no area of constitutional law today where the citizen can expect so little help from the courts as if he has a claim that his right to privacy under the Fourth Amendment has been breached.

Given the reluctance of the courts to enforce the Fourth Amendment in areas it plainly encompasses, there seems little likelihood it will be invoked to govern great intrusions in privacy never envisioned by its authors. In fits and starts, the courts have been willing to enjoin some forms of electronic eavesdropping under the banner of the Fourth Amendment and, even more rarely, some lower courts have invoked it against psychological questionnaires and lie detectors. But it is not a promising path for anyone interested in finding a way to curb most forms of dossier-building.

Other constitutional avenues are being explored, though not yet with any great success. The First Amendment's guarantees of freedom of expression and assembly are occasionally applied to the collection of data on political views and associations. The Fifth Amendment's guarantee of due process of law encompasses the presumption of innocence. A handful of court decisions have blocked the dissemination of arrest records not followed by convictions in an effort to make the presumption meaningful. And in a 1965 Supreme Court case, several justices found a protection for privacy in the Ninth Amendment: "The enumeration in this Constitution, of certain rights, shall not be construed to deny or disparage others retained by the people." The case, *Griswold v. Connecticut,* overturned a law against the use of contraceptive devices because it interfered with the privacy of the marital relationship. Citing the narrow protections for privacy derived from other amendments to the Constitution (including the Third Amendment's prohibition against compulsory quartering of soldiers in private homes in time of peace), the justices said that together, the Constitution forms a "penumbra" guaranteeing privacy. The Ninth Amendment guaranteed in broader terms rights such as privacy emanating "from the totality of the constitutional scheme under which we live," as Justice Brandeis stated it a generation earlier.

Despite the sweeping protection for privacy suggested by *Griswold*, its principles have rarely been followed. *Griswold* was the high water mark of the Warren Court's expansive reading of the Bill of Rights. In the intervening decade, the courts have backed away from the Ninth Amendment and its potential as a protection for privacy.

The word "privacy" never appears in the Constitution. It is only in the last century that this word has been used as a legal concept to describe the state's duty to let people alone. An 1890 article by Louis D. Brandeis and Samuel D. Warren on "The Right to Privacy" helped arouse interest. Many years later, as a justice of the Supreme Court, Brandeis championed privacy in one of the dissenting opinions for which he is principally remembered today. "The right to be let alone," said Brandeis in *Olmstead v. United States* in 1928, is "the most comprehensive of rights and the right most valued by civilized men." But he couldn't persuade a majority of his colleagues. Chief Justice Taft's opinion for the Court upheld the wiretapping of Olmstead, a bootlegger during Prohibition, because no "tangible" property had been seized and the eavesdropping was accomplished without a physical invasion of his property.

Wiretapping and lie detectors provoked most legal debates about privacy prior to the 1960s. The few efforts to challenge dossier-building practices in the courts have been rebuffed. Judges resist the use of constitutional provisions to curb dossiers. Necessarily, advocates of controls must turn to Congress and the state legislatures. And that means public opinion must demand curbs.

"Americans, most of whom have never suffered the indignities of police state invasions of their rights, have little fear of government dossiers—not just on criminals, but on them," said a Roper organization survey in early 1974. "The vast majority think it 'appropriate' for the FBI to have on file about people like themselves such information as fingerprints, race, and birth date. They also think the FBI should have prison records, and arrests resulting in convictions . . . just over half of the public thinks the FBI should have psychiatric histories." There are some limits on the information Americans think should be collected. Only 39 percent of Americans said the FBI should have records of arrests that do not result in convictions, and only 21 percent would allow the FBI to collect opinions of neighbors about individuals' moral character.

Americans are much less tolerant of data collection by private employers. Fifty percent would allow private employers access to conviction records, 38 percent to psychiatric records, and only 20 percent to records of arrests not resulting in convictions. By far the greatest resistance to data collection appears in response to questions about credit card companies. Only 15 percent of Americans would give them access to conviction records, 10 percent to psychiatric records, and a mere 8 percent would let credit card companies see records of arrests that don't lead to convictions. While the Roper survey does not exactly contradict George Bernard Shaw's insistence that Americans have no sense of privacy, neither is it cause for abject despair.

The public's willingness to allow the FBI to collect personal data reflects the bureau's success in portraying itself as a no-nonsense law enforcement investigative agency. Americans would be less tolerant if they knew that the FBI as a data collector serves employment agency and credit bureau purposes more effectively than it does the investigation of crime. And, it is good news indeed that most Americans have sufficient faith in the presumption of innocence to oppose giving records of arrests not resulting in convictions to anyone, including the FBI.

One disturbing finding by the Roper survey is the low regard for the confidentiality of psychiatric records. Still, only about half as many approve of collecting information about sexual history as psychiatric history: 24 percent approve of the FBI collecting sexual history, 51 percent psychiatric history; 5 percent approve of a credit card company collecting sexual history, 10 percent psychiatric history. These results suggest that references to psychiatric history conjure up images of psychopathic criminals or at least someone other than oneself—everyone has a sexual history. Occasional sensational publicity on crimes committed by ex–mental patients is highly misleading. Ironically, individuals who were patients in mental hospitals commit crimes much less often than other people do. If investigation of crime is the most widely accepted rationale for data-collection, logically, records on ex–psychiatric hospital patients should be compiled less readily than records on those never hospitalized.

Privacy is often, mistakenly, perceived as a predominantly middle-class concern. The Roper survey demonstrates that non-whites accurately gauge how much of a stake they have in limiting dossiers. Nonwhites disapproved of the collecting of information about twice as often as whites.

Resistance to data collection is greatest when people feel that irrelevant data about their private lives influences their economic transactions. Blacks experience the use of irrelevant data against them much more often than whites.

The most important economic transaction most of us ever engage in is getting a job. We grow up believing, as the Bible tells, that, "In the sweat of thy brow shalt thou eat bread." What Richard Nixon called the "work ethic" and what we used to call the "Protestant ethic" dominates our society. Work, said Freud, gives a person a "place in a portion of reality." It also pays the bills.

Proposals for limiting the accumulation of dossiers should focus on protecting the right to work. That purpose would be served best if all dossiers described in this book were assembled in one place and a fire set to the lot of them. Since such a drastic, simple, and effective approach is impractical at best, legal safeguards must substitute.

First, a warning: that word "safeguard" is dangerous. It implies that an instrument which can cause a great deal of evil can be so controlled that it causes only good. Usually, it doesn't work out that way. Man's capacity to devise safeguards is exceeded by his capacity to devise loopholes which defeat safeguards. A safeguard implies that its main effect is good. That is often quite untrue. Certainly, it is in this instance. The main effect of dossiers is baneful. Their purpose is to track what people have been doing with their lives, especially, what someone else thinks is bad. Even if dossiers are never used against a person, they restrict the sense of freedom. We know or suspect that institutions employ clerks whose job it is to prevent us from exceeding the limits set for us by our records. We lower our sights, in consequence, and conform to the dossiers.

When, at a 1973 meeting sponsored by the American Bar Association, I called for the destruction of dossiers, I was challenged by a Kansas prison warden. He argued for maintenance of records because the "records are earned." They are an important part of punishment for doing wrong, he said.

The Kansas prison warden made the most honest argument for keeping dossiers. Records kept and disseminated by such presumably benevolent institutions as schools and mental hospitals do not help the people they label, despite that avowed purpose. Nor do the records maintained by law enforcement agencies serve the investigative purposes claimed for them. They punish people, though the dossier compilers seldom admit this is the purpose or acknowledge that it is the consequence. Because they have such enormous punitive impact on their direct and indirect victims, I want to destroy the dossiers.

I do not apologize for taking such an "extreme" position. Some things warrant extreme positions. As a character in Herman Melville's novel, *The Confidence Man,* puts it to one who does not share his own abolitionist and, therefore, extreme sentiments against slavery: "Picked and prudent sentiments. You are the moderate man, the invaluable understrapper of the wicked man. You, the moderate man, may be used for wrong, but you are useless for right."

Most stigmas people acquire are pinned to them very early in life. This is one of the most important reasons for destroying records, it seems to me. School, predelinquency, and juvenile court records, and records of drug addiction afflict the young. Selective Service and military discharge records label the young. In 1971, 53.6 percent of all arrests were of persons under 25. Of all the stigmas described in this book, only confinement in mental hospitals fails to afflict the young disproportionately.

Dossiers are maintained in the belief that people who make trouble are irredeemable. That notion is contradicted by the natural and precipitous decline in troublemaking as people reach maturity. Elimination of the records would allow people to leave behind them the stormy years of youth. They would have the opportunity to enjoy the benefits our society has to offer. The end of records would help them adopt styles of life less threatening to the tranquility of the rest of us.

But, since life is real and earnest, I suppose that the dream of a grand bonfire must be postponed.

A frequent proposal for curbing the use of criminal conviction records is to seal them, after a period of years. The biblically significant period of seven years turns up in bills introduced in Congress and in the state legislatures. Examination of what happens to exconvicts suggests that sealing records after seven years would benefit very few.

An FBI report on 18,567 offenders who had been released in 1963 showed that after three years 52.6 percent had been rearrested; after the fourth year, 60.9 percent; after five years it rose only slightly to 63.3 percent; and at the end of the sixth year it had only risen to 65.1 percent, an addition of just 1.8 percent. The study supports the common-sense proposition that an exconvict needs the most help right after he has gotten out of prison. If he hasn't been rearrested for six or seven years after getting out of prison, chances are he has rehabilitated himself or is so skillful a criminal that he doesn't get caught or that he is dead. Sealing the record of such a person makes little sense.

If a record is to be sealed or destroyed, it should be done immediately: right after acquittal, when a person gets out of prison or leaves a mental hospital.

The right to examine one's own record and challenge its accuracy is frequently proposed. If anecdotal records compiled by schools, mental hospitals, and credit bureaus were accessible to those whose names are on the file folders, the compilers would hesitate before including gossipy or false information, or unfair interpretations.

Access to one's own arrest records would allow the person not convicted to insure that the disposition accompanies his arrest record. An absolute prohibition on the maintenance and dissemination of arrest records that did not include disposition records would be more useful. Even better, would be a prohibition on keeping and distributing records of arrest of those never convicted.

The New York State Identification and Intelligence System permits people to examine their own arrest records. It works like this. A person goes to an office of NYSIIS in one of the state's major cities and submits his fingerprints. The prints are checked by computer against the six million in the NYSIIS data bank and, in a matter of moments, a printout informs the person of the record maintained on him.

Only a handful of people have taken advantage of the right to see the records maintained on them by NYSIIS, and no wonder. Not many people are willing to give a law enforcement agency their fingerprints in order to find out their records. It is the only way to get the facts, however, since this is how the NYSIIS files are organized. It is also the only way so far available to be sure the person sees his own record and not somebody else's.

The fingerprint data banks maintained by law enforcement agencies are, mostly, fairly accurate—incomplete and misleading because of their failure to note dispositions, but accurate. For a person with a record of arrest or conviction, the important thing is not to be judged by that record when seeking a job. Even the right to check or to complete the record may be insufficient because employers may be as reluctant to hire people acquitted of crimes as people who were convicted.

A giant step forward would be a prohibition on the maintenance of all arrest records not resulting in convictions. Most Western European countries do not maintain arrest records, though exceptions are made when a person already has a conviction record and then is arrested again but not convicted a second time. "In the event of acquittal," says a recent book on British practices,

the police generally destroy the data. . . . Some criminal record office spokesmen . . . insist that no form of "black mark" remains in their records as the result of acquittal. Other criminal record offices do retain certain information generated in prosecutions leading to acquittals . . . information may be retained after acquittal if the charges have involved matters considered by the police especially serious or especially likely to be repeated, sexual offenses being the prime example. . . .[1]

In the United States, it would simply not do to allow this much discretion in record maintenance. Unless there is express prohibition in law of the maintenance of arrest records, they will be maintained. And, if there are to be exceptions, a notion which flies in the face of the presumption of innocence, they too must be precisely described in the law. A loose restriction such as

1. James B. Rule, *Private Lives and Public Surveillance* (New York: Schocken Books 1974), p. 67.

"dangerousness" would be interpreted out of existence. If legislators are to insist on the maintenance of arrest records of persons charged with child molestation or rape, those exact crimes should be spelled out in law. It will be difficult enough to get law enforcement agencies to comply with any laws restricting record keeping; imprecision will greatly compound the problem.

Laws which limit the dissemination of information, as opposed to their collection, are attractive, but of questionable value. Once an information data bank exists, incentives to get access to it appear. Sometimes restrictions on dissemination fail because administrators are corrupt. Examples are the White House's use of Internal Revenue Service data on its political opponents and the FBI's leaks to one of the bureau's principal congressional champions, John Rooney, of embarrassing data on his political opponents. Or, a legislature may simply drop the restrictions under pressure of some economic interest. The bill adopted by Congress to overturn Judge Gesell's decision restricting FBI dissemination of arrest records to law enforcement agencies was sponsored by Senators Bible and Cannon of Nevada. They were representing the interest of their state's gaming industry in access to the records. The New York law giving that state's securities industry access to the state's criminal records system to screen employees was lobbied through by the industry to counter bad publicity about losses of stocks. The securities firms sought to shift the blame for their losses, which resulted from sloppiness, to thieves they were first going to detect by fingerprinting their employees. The realities of bureaucratic practice also limit the value of restrictions on dissemination. The British criminal record offices, for example,

answer hundreds of telephone requests each day—the figure is in the thousands for the Metropolitan [London] office. . . . It is impossible to prevent in all cases the dissemination of such information to non-police callers, even though criminal record office staffs may do their best to do so. Virtually anyone familiar with the telephone number of the regional office and the routines for making such requests can eventually obtain the information he seeks: if not on the first try, then sooner or later. The vulnerability of these offices is especially great to former members of the police, who are invariably well versed in the techniques of making such requests. . . .[2]

In the United States, also, industrial security jobs are dominated by ex-FBI agents and expolicemen. Their training and their old friendships with colleagues still in law enforcement agencies get them the cooperation of those agencies.

It is impossible to police each agency privileged to receive data. Even if the FBI were to restrict the dissemination of arrest and conviction data to other law enforcement agencies, how could thousands of recipient police departments be checked to see they don't disseminate it further? The simple answer is that it is not possible. That is one reason the FBI has never even tried.

An important reform would be a requirement that an agency which maintains a dossier notify the subject of the dossier every time it gives out information. The person could then counter discreditable information. If an arrest is reported, the person could explain the circumstances. If it is a bad credit rating, the person could explain that the merchandise was defective and, therefore, he refused to pay for it. If it is a school's account of radical political activities, the person could go to court to challenge the use of such data for employment purposes because it puts an improper price on the exercise of First Amendment rights.

Notification has been opposed because it is too "difficult" or "expensive." It is hard to take such arguments very seriously. As long as data are forwarded from one institution to another, it should be neither difficult nor expensive to send a copy to the person's last known address.

2. Ibid., p. 82.

A less satisfactory procedure, though still a valuable reform, would require agencies disseminating personal data to publish guides to their procedures. A guide would contain a description of the data collected; the kinds of persons about whom they are collected; the sources of the data; the persons and agencies with access to the data; the circumstances of access; and the procedures that should be followed by someone who wants to see his own record and, if need be, correct it. A requirement that such guides be published would impose only minimal burdens on data collectors and, except for their desire to remain unaccountable, it is hard to imagine grounds for opposing it.

Another significant reform would limit the use of data. A law could prohibit the use of arrest records as a criterion for employment or continuing employment. On its face, such a law would be attractive. If there is a significant investigative purpose served by arrest records, which I very much doubt, that purpose could still be served. At the same time, at least in theory, the records would not deny people jobs.

The difficulty comes in practice. If arrest records are readily available, a law saying they cannot be considered in hiring would be hard to enforce. Most decisions about whom to hire are necessarily subjective. It would be difficult to demonstrate that an arrest record led to the denial of a job. Only if it is used as a complement to a restriction on the dissemination of data would there be any great value in a law barring consideration of data.

The safeguards I have discussed have limitations when considered alone; in combination they would have beneficial impact.[3]

There is a growing public awareness that something ought to be done. It was expressed by President Ford in his address to a

---

3. Such safeguards were proposed in an omnibus congressional bill to protect privacy sponsored by Representatives Barry Goldwater, Jr., and Edward Koch. They were also proposed in "Records, Computers, and the Rights of Citizens," a 1973 report by the Secretary's Advisory Committee on Automated Personal Data Systems of the U.S. Department of Health, Education and Welfare.

joint session of Congress just three days after he became president. "There will be no illegal tapings, eavesdropping, buggings, or break-ins by my Administration," said Ford. "There will be hot pursuit of tough laws to prevent illegal invasions of privacy in both government and private activities."

Ford's statement raises the hope that the national revulsion against Watergate may provide the sense of urgency needed to translate proposals for privacy laws into reality. In a nation preoccupied with the pressing problem of safety, many had believed that privacy was a luxury that must be sacrificed to achieve that greater good.

Many of the dossier-building practices described in this book are motivated by the desire for safety, yet they have helped to create the very social dislocation and crime they are intended to combat. Millions of persons are labeled as pariahs by their records. The label is self-fulfilling. Unable to get jobs or housing, harassed by officialdom, they have become pariahs.

It is urgent that we bring back into the social mainstream the millions of these rootless and disaffected people. We can recapture many for a constructive life. Our best hope is to stop adding to the pariah population. We can end the labeling of children as "disruptive" or "mentally deficient." We can stop classifying people by their arrests or "undesirable" discharges from the armed forces. We can end the dossiers of misdeeds, real and alleged, that follow us and our children everywhere.

Appendix

Discharge Dossiers

SPN NUMBERS AND DEFINITIONS

Procedures For Requesting Deletion of Abbreviated Separation
(SPN) from Discharge Document

Veterans who wish to have their Separation Program Number (SPN), or Separation Designation Number (SDN), Reason and Authority for discharge, and Reenlistment Code deleted from their copy of the DD Form 214, "Report of Separation From Active Duty," (or from previous editions of the form) may apply to their former service to have the abbreviated codes deleted from their copy of the form. Requests should be mailed to the following addresses:

Army:
Commander
Reserve Components Personnel and
   Administration Center
Box 12479
Olivette Branch
St. Louis, Missouri 63132

Air Force:
*Air Force Military Personnel Center
   (DPMDR)
Randolph AFB, Texas 78148

(*It is preferable that former USAF members make their request through a local base personnel office.)

Navy:
Chief
Bureau of Naval Personnel (Pers 38)
Department of the Navy
Washington, D.C. 20370

Marine Corps:
Commandant
U.S. Marine Corps (MSRB - 10)
Headquarters, U.S. Marine Corps
Washington, D. C. 20380

• 200

The request should include name, social security number, any military service identification number, dates of service, and a copy of the DD Form 214.

Further information is available at local military personnel offices.

If a number other than one listed below appears in box 11c of your DD Form 214, contact the Lawyers Military Defense Committee of the American Civil Liberties Union Foundation, Dupont Circle Building, Suite 604, 1346 Connecticut Avenue, N.W., Washington, D.C. 20036. Other numbers were in occasional use.

Revised Enlisted Separation Program Numbers & Definitions

201 —Enlisted Personnel—Expiration of term of service (includes personnel on ADT as initial trainees).

21L—Enlisted Personnel—Separation for good and sufficient reason when determined by secretarial authority.

21T—Enlisted Personnel—Release of REP 63 trainees due to emergency conditions. (Does not apply to active duty).

21U—Separation for failure to demonstrate adequate potential for promotion.

202 —Expiration of term of enlistment.

203 —Expiration of term of active obligation service.

205 —Release from active and transferred to reserve.

212 —Honorable wartime service subsequent to desertion.

213 —Discharge for retirement as an officer.

214 —To accept commission as an officer in the Army, or to accept recall to active duty as an Army Reserve officer.

215 —To accept appointment as war-rant officer in the Army, or to accept recall to active duty as Army Reserve warrant officer.

217 —To accept commission or appointment in the Armed Forces of the United States (other than Army).

219 —Erroneous induction

220 —Marriage, female only.

221 —Pregnancy.

222 —Parenthood.

225 —Minority.

226 —Dependency.

227 —Hardship.

229 —Surviving family members.

230 —Retirement after 20 years but less than 30 years' active Federal service.

231 —Retirement after 30 years' active Federal service.

238 —Service retirement in lieu of other administrative action.

240 —Unconditional resignation of enlisted personnel serving on unspecified enlistment.

241 —Resignation of enlisted personnel on unspecified enlistment in lieu of reduction for misconduct or inefficiency.

242 —Resignation of enlisted person-

nel on unspecified enlistment for the good of the service.

243 —Resignation of enlisted personnel on unspecified enlistment in lieu of board of action when based on unfitness.

244 —Resignation of enlisted personnel on unspecified in lieu of board action when based on unsuitability.

245 —Resignation of enlisted personnel on unspecified enlistment in lieu of separation for disloyalty or subversion.

246 —Discharge for the good of the service.

247 —Unsuitability/multiple reasons.

248 —Unsuitability.

249 —Resignation of enlisted personnel on unspecified enlistment (homosexual).

250 —Punitive discharge, class I homosexual, general court-martial.

251 —Punitive discharge, class II homosexual, general court-martial.

252 —Punitive discharge, class I homosexual, special court-martial.

253 —Discharged as a result of board action (class II homosexual). Rescinded.

255 —Retirement in lieu of discharge under AR635–89 (homosexuality).

256 —Acceptance of discharge in lieu of board action (class III homosexual). Rescinded.

257 —Unfitness, homosexual acts.

258 —Unfitness/multiple reasons.

260 —Unsuitability/inaptitude.

261 —Psychiatric or psychoneurotic disorder.

262 —Unsuitability/enuresis.

263 —Enuresis.

264 —Unsuitability/character and behavior disorders.

265 —Character disorders.

270 —Placed on Temporary Disability Retired List.

271 —Permanently retired by reason of physical disability.

273 —Physical disability with entitlement to receive severance pay.

274 —Physical disability resulting from intentional misconduct or willful neglect or incurred during period of unauthorized absence. Not entitled to severance pay.

276 —Released from EAD and revert to retired list prior to ETS.

277 —Physical disability, EPTS, established by medical board. Discharged by reason of physical disability upon application by individual. Not entitled to severance pay.

278 —Physical disability, EPTS, established by physical evaluation board proceedings. Not entitled to severance pay.

279 —Release from EAD and revert to retired list at ETS.

28B —Unfitness, frequent involvement in incidents of a discreditable nature with civil or military authorities.

28E —Financial irresponsibility.

28F —Unfitness, an established pattern showing dishonorable failure to pay just debts.

28G —Unfitness, an established pattern for showing dishonorable failure to contribute adequate support to dependents or failure to comply with order, decrees, or judgments of a civil court concerning support of dependents.

281 —Unsanitary habits.

280 —Misconduct/fraudulent entry into the Army.

282 —Misconduct/prolonged unauthorized absence for more than 1 year desertion.

283 —Misconduct/AWOL, trial waived or deemed inadvisable.

284 —Misconduct/convicted or adjudged a juvenile offender by a civil court during current term of active military service.

285 —Initially adjudged a juvenile offender by a civil court during current term of active military service. Rescinded.

286 —Repeated military offenses not warranting trial by court-martial.

287 —Unclean habits, including repeated venereal disease.

288 —Habits and traits of character manifested by anti-social, amoral trends.

289 —Unsuitability/alcoholism.

290 —Desertion (court-martial).

292 —Other than desertion (court-martial).

293 —General court-martial.

294 —Special court-martial.

311 —Alien without legal residence in the United States.

312 —Separation of members of Reserve components on active duty who, due to age, would be precluded from attaining eligi-

bility pay as provided by 10 USC 1331–1337.

313 —To immediately enlist or reenlist.

314 —Importance to National health, safety or interest.

316 —Release, lack of jurisdiction.

318 —Conscientious objection.

319 —Erroneous enlistment.

320 —To accept employment with a legally established law enforcement agency.

333 —Discharge of Cuban volunteers upon completion of specified training. Rescinded.

344 —Release of Cuban volunteers upon completion of specified training. Rescinded.

361 —Homosexual tendencies.

362 —Unsuitability/homosexual tendencies, desires, or interest, but without overt homosexual acts, in service.

367 —Aggressive reaction.

368 —Anti-social personality.

369 —Cyclothymic personality.

370 —Released from EAD by reason of physical disability and revert to inactive status for the purpose of retirement under title 10, USC sections 1331–1337, in lieu of discharge with entitlement to receive severance pay.

375 —Discharge because of not meeting medical fitness standards at time of enlistment.

376 —Release from Military Control (void induction) because of not meeting medical fitness standards at time of induction.

377–Non-fulfillment of enlistment commitment.

38A–Desertion/trial deemed inadvisable (WWII). Rescinded.

38B–Desertion/trial deemed inadvisable (Peacetime desertion). Rescinded.

38C–Desertion/trial deemed inadvisable (Korean War) Rescinded.

380–Desertion/trial barred by 10, USC, section 834 (Art. 34, UCMJ). Rescinded.

381–Desertion/trial deemed inadvisable (Spanish-American War/WWI) Rescinded.

383–Criminalism.

384–Unfitness/drug abuse, as defined in para 6a (3), AR 635-212.

385–Pathological lying.

386–Unfitness/an established pattern for shirking.

387–Habits and traits of character manifested by misconduct.

388–Unfitness/sexual perversions, including but not limited to lewd and lascivious acts, indecent exposure, indecent acts with or assault upon a child, or other indecent acts and offenses.

41A–Apathy, lack of interest.

41C–To accept a teaching position.

41D–Discharge of enlisted personnel on unspecified enlistment who completed 20 years' active Federal service, do not submit application for retirement; Commander determines discharge will be in best interest of the Government.

41E–Obesity.

411–Early separation of oversea returnee.

412–Enlisted members of medical holding detachments or units who, upon completion of hospitalization, do not intend to immediately enlist or reenlistment in the Regular Army.

413–To enter or return to college, university, or equivalent educational institution.

414–To accept or return to employment of a seasonal nature.

415–Early release of inductees who have served on active duty prior to their present tour of duty.

416–Physical disqualification for duty in MOS.

418–Discharge of enlisted personnel on unspecified enlistment who complete 30 years' active Federal service and do not submit application for retirement.

419–Discharge of enlisted personnel on unspecified enlistment over 55 years of age who have completed 20 years' active Federal service and do not submit application for retirement.

420–Discharge or release of individuals with less than 3 months remaining to serve who fail to continue as students (academic failure) at service academies.

421–Early release at Christmas will be issued as appropriate by Army and has been included in separation edit table. Rescinded.

422–Early release at original ETS of enlisted personnel who have executed a voluntary extension. Rescinded.

423–Early release after original ETS

of personnel serving on a voluntary extension. Rescinded.

424 —Separation at ETS after completing a period of voluntary extension. Rescinded.

425 —Discharge (inductees) to enlist for Warrant Officer Flight Training.

426 —Discharge (inductees) to enlist to attend critical MOS school.

427 —Discharge (inductees) to enlist for Officer Candidate School.

428 —Discharge for failure to complete Officer Candidate School.

429 —Discharge because of not meeting medical fitness standards for flight training.

430 —Early separation of personnel denied reenlistment under Qualitative Management Program.

431 —Reduction in authorized strength.

432 —Early release to serve one year in an ARNG or USAR unit.

433 —Involuntary release of personnel on compassionate assignment.

434 —Early release of AUS and first term RA personnel—phase down release programs. (Early out from Vietnam)

436 —Reduction in strength—USASA option/First Term.

437 —AUS, RA First Term, exempted from 90 day suspension of Early Release Program for reasons for intolerable personal problems.

440 —Separation for concealment of serious arrest record.

46A—Unsuitability, apathy, defective attitudes and inability to expend effort constructively.

46B —Sexual deviate.

46C—Apathy/obesity.

46D—Sexual deviate.

460 —Emotional instability reaction.

461 —Inadequate personality.

462 —Mental deficiency.

463 —Paranoid personality.

464 —Schizoid personality.

469 —Unsuitability.

480 —Personality disorders.

482 —Desertion/trial barred by 10, USC, sec. 843 (Art. 43, UCMJ). Rescinded.

488 —Unsuitability (general discharge separation).

489 —Military Personnel Security Program (disloyal or subversive).

500 —Resignation—hardship.

501 —Resignation—National health, safety, or interest.

502 —Resignation—completion of required service.

503 —Resignation—enlistment in the Regular Army—Regular Officer.

504 —Resignation—withdrawal of ecclesiastical indorsement.

505 —Resignation—serving under a suspended sentence to dismissal.

508 —Resignation—to attend school.

509 —Resignation—in lieu of elimination because of substandard or unsatisfactory performance of duty.

510 —Resignation—interest of National security (in lieu of elimination).

511 —Resignation—in lieu of elimination (homosexuality).

518 —Resignation—in lieu of elimination because of unfitness or unacceptable conduct.

522 —Resignation—in lieu of elimination because of conduct triable by courts-martial or in lieu thereof.

524 —Resignation—unqualified or other miscellaneous reasons.

528 —Resignation—marriage.

529 —Resignation—pregnancy.

530 —Resignation—parenthood (minor children).

536 —Voluntary discharge (substandard performance of duty).

537 —Involuntary discharge—unfitness (unacceptable conduct).

539 —Voluntary discharge—termination of RA or AUS warrant or member serving on active duty in RA or AUS warrant to retire in commissioned status.

545 —Involuntary discharge—failure of selection for permanent promotion (commissioned officers).

546 —Involuntary discharge—failure of selection for permanent promotion (warrant officer).

550 —Involuntary discharge—reasons as specified by HDQA.

551 —Involuntary discharge—Administrative discharge, GCM.

552 —Dismissal—General court-martial (homosexual).

554 —Dismissal—General Court-martial.

555 —Involuntary discharge—failure to complete basic, company officer, or associate company officer course—USAR officers.

556 —Failure to complete basic, company officer, or associate company officer course—ARNGUS officers.

558 —Voluntary discharge—conscientious objection.

586 —Involuntary discharge—for reasons involving board action or in lieu thereof (homosexual).

588 —Involuntary discharge—reasons involving board action, or in lieu thereof—unfitness or unacceptable conduct.

589 —Voluntary discharge—reasons involving board action, or in lieu thereof, due to substandard performance of duty.

590 —Involuntary discharge—Interest of National security.

595 —Involuntary discharge—pregnancy.

596 —Involuntary discharge—parenthood (minor children).

597 —Voluntary discharge—administrative.

599 —Voluntary REFRAD—lack of jurisdiction.

600 —Voluntary REFRAD—to enlist in Regular Army.

601 —Voluntary REFRAD—to enlist in Regular Army for purpose of retirement.

602 —Voluntary REFRAD—National health, safety, or interest.

603 —Involuntary REFRAD—due to disapproval of request for extension of service.

604 —Voluntary REFRAD—Hardship.

606 —Voluntary REFRAD—dual status officer to revert to regular Warrant Officer.

609 —Voluntary REFRAD—to attend school or accept a teaching position.

610 —Voluntary REFRAD—marriage.

611 —Voluntary REFRAD—expiration of active duty commitment, voluntarily serving on active duty.

612 —Voluntary REFRAD—expiration of active duty commitment, involuntarily serving on active duty.

616 —Voluntary REFRAD—selection for entrance to a service academy.

618—Voluntary REFRAD—in lieu of serving in lower grade than Reserve grade.

619 —Voluntary REFRAD—by request, includes MC and DC officers.

620 —Voluntary REFRAD—interdepartmental transfer of other than Medical officers.

621 —Voluntary REFRAD—in lieu of unqualified resignation.

623 —Voluntary REFRAD—interdepartmental transfer of Medical officers.

624 —Voluntary REFRAD—Release from ADT to enter on 24 months active duty.

625 —Voluntary REFRAD—Annual screening, voluntary release prior to 90th day subsequent to receipt of notification.

627 —Involuntary REFRAD—maximum age.

631 —Involuntary REFRAD—failure of selection for permanent reserve promotion (discharged).

632 —Involuntary REFRAD—failure of selection for permanent reserve promotion (commission retained).

633 —Involuntary REFRAD—failure of selection for promotion, temporary.

640 —Involuntary REFRAD—commissioned officer under sentence of dismissal and warrant officer under sentence of dishonorable discharge awaiting appellate review.

644 —Voluntary and Involuntary REFRAD—convenience of Government, or as specified by Secretary of the Army.

645 —Involuntary REFRAD—annual screening, release on 90th day subsequent to receipt of notification.

646 —Involuntary REFRAD—maximum service, warrant officers.

647 —Involuntary REFRAD—maximum service, commissioned officers.

648 —Involuntary REFRAD—completion of prescribed years of service.

649 —Involuntary REFRAD—withdrawal of esslesiastical indorsement.

650 —Involuntary REFRAD—physically disqualified upon order to active duty.

651 —Involuntary REFRAD—release of reserve unit and return to reserve status.

652 —Involuntary REFRAD—release of unit of NG or NG (US) and return to state control.

655 —Involuntary REFRAD—revert to retired list, not by reason of physical disability.

657 —Involuntary REFRAD—physical

disability. revert to inactive status for purpose of retirement under chapter 67, 10 USC in lieu of discharge with entitlement to receive disability severance pay.

660 —Physical disability discharge —entitlement to severance pay.

661 —Physical disability discharge— disability resulting from intentional misconduct, or willful neglect or incurred during a period of unauthorized absence. Not entitled to receive disability severance pay.

662 —Physical disability discharge— EPTS, established by physical evaluation board. Not entitled to disability severance pay.

668 —Dropped from rolls—AWOL, conviction and confinement by civil authorities.

669 —Dropped from rolls—AWOL, desertion.

672 —Involuntary REFRAD—Medical service personnel who receive unfavorable background investigation and/or National Agency Check.

681 —Voluntary REFRAD—to accept employment with a legally established law enforcement agency.

685 —Resignation—failure to meet medical fitness standards at time of appointment.

686 —Involuntary discharge—failure to resign under chap. 16, AR 635-120, when determined to be in the best interests of the Government and the individual.

689 —Voluntary REFRAD—reduction in strength, voluntary release prior to 90th day subsequent to receipt of notification.

690 —Involuntary REFRAD—reduction in strength, release on 90th day subsequent to receipt of notification.

70A—Mandatory retirement—35 years service/5 years in grade, Regular Army major general.

70B—Mandatory retirement—age 62, Regular Army major general.

70C—Mandatory retirement—age 60, Regular Army major general whose retirement has been deferred.

70D—Mandatory retirement—age 64, Regular Army major general whose retirement has been deferred and each permanent professor and the Registrar of the US Military Academy.

70E—Mandatory retirement—30 years service/5 years in grade, Regular Army brigadier general.

70F—Mandatory retirement—30 years of service/5 years in grade, Regular colonels.

70G—Mandatory retirement—28 years service/Regular lieutenant colonels.

70J —Mandatory retirement—age 60, regular commissioned officers below major general.

70K—Mandatory retirement—more than 30 years active service, professors US Military Academy.

70L—Mandatory retirement—30 years or more active service, Regular warrant officers.

70M –Mandatory retirement–age 62, Regular warrant officers.

701 –Enlisted separation–early release of personnel assigned to installations or units scheduled for inactivation, permanent change of station, or demobilization.

741 –Mandatory retirement–failure of selection for promotion, established retirement date, commissioned Officer.

742–Mandatory retirement–failure of selection for promotion, established retirement date, warrant officer.

743 –Enlisted separation–early release of personnel upon release of unit of the ARNG or the ARNGUS from active Federal service and return to State control.

744 –Mandatory retirement–failure of selection for promotion, early retirement date, commissioned officers.

745 –Mandatory retirement–failure of selection for promotion, early retirement date, warrant officers.

747 –Mandatory retirement–failure of selection for promotion, retained for retirement, commissioned officer.

748 –Mandatory retirement–failure of selection for promotion, retained for retirement, warrant officer.

749 –Enlisted separation–early release of Puerto Rican personnel who fail to quality for training.

753 –Enlisted separation–early release of reserve personnel upon release of Reserve units.

764 –Enlisted separation–release of REP 63 trainees upon completion of MOS training.

77E –Mandatory retirement–surplus in grade after 30 years service, removal from active list (Regular Army).

77J –Voluntary retirement–placement on retired list at age 60.

77M –Mandatory retirement–permanent retirement by reason of physical disability.

77N –Mandatory retirement–placed on Temporary Disability Retired List.

77P –Voluntary retirement–in lieu of or as a result of elimination board proceedings. Regular Army and Reserve commissioned officers and warrant officers.

77Q –Mandatory retirement–Temporary Disability Retirement in lieu of or as a result of elimination proceedings.

77R –Mandatory retirement–permanent disability retirement in lieu of or as a result of elimination proceedings.

77S –Voluntary retirement–Regular Army and Reserve commissioned officer.

77T –Voluntary retirement–Regular Army and Reserve warrant officers.

77U –Voluntary retirement–Regular Army commissioned officers with 30 or more years of service.

77V –Voluntary retirement–enlisted

personnel, voluntarily retired as a commissioned officer.

77W–Voluntary retirement—enlisted personnel, voluntarily retired as a warrant officer.

77X–Voluntary retirement—warrant officer voluntarily retired as a commissioned officer.

77Y–Mandatory retirement—retirement of Director of Music, USMA, as the President may direct.

77Z–Mandatory retirement—Regular Army commissioned officers with WWI Service.

771 –Mandatory retirement—commissioned officers, unfitness or substandard performance of duty.

772 –Mandatory retirement—warrants officers, unfitness or substandard performance of duty.

78A–Mandatory retirement—formerly retired other than for disability who while on active duty incurred a disability of at least 30 percent.

78B–Mandatory retirement—formerly retired for disability who while on active duty suffered aggravation of disability for which he was formerly retired.

79A–Voluntary REFRAD—as USAR warrant officer (aviator) to accept USAR commission (aviator) with concurrent active duty.

79B–Resignation—as RA WO (aviator) to accept USAR commission (aviator) with concurrent active duty.

941 –Dropped from rolls (as deserter).

942 –Dropped from rolls (as military prisoner).

943 –Dropped from rolls (as missing or captured).

944 –Battle casualty.

945 –Death (non-battle—resulting from disease).

946 –Death (non-battle—resulting from other than disease).

947 –Current term of service voided as fraudulently enlisted while AWOL from prior service.

948 –to enter US Military Academy.

949 –to enter any of the service academies (other than USMA).

971 –Erroneously reported as returned from dropped from rolls as deserter (previously reported under transaction GA).

972 –Erroneously reported as restored to duty from dropped from rolls as military prisoner (previously reported under transaction code GB).

973–Erroneously reported as returned from dropped from rolls as missing or captured (previously reported under transaction code GC).

976 –Minority, void enlistment or induction—enlisted personnel.

Index

Ability grouping, 28-35
American Civil Liberties Union (ACLU), 11-12, 24, 45, 79-80, 87, 91, 98-99, 160-62. *See also* specific states
Adams, John, 186
Addlestone, David, 78, 91
Agitator Detector, Inc., 155
Agriculture, Department of, 14
Ahsaf, Carmen (*Ahsaf v. Nyquist*), 65-67
Aid to Dependent Children, 183
Aiken, Thomas, Jr., 83-84
Air force, 14-15, 78, 85, 200
AJJUST, 161
Alabama, University of, 154
Alaska, 130
Albuquerque, N. Mexico, 16, 130, 131
Alcoholics, 61
American Agent, 126n
American Bankers Ass'n, 101-2
American Bar Ass'n, 111, 112, 192
American Correctional Ass'n, 115
American Federation of Teachers, 32
American Management Ass'n, 62
American Psychiatric Ass'n, 46
American Psychological Ass'n, 46
American Sociological Ass'n, 46
Anderson, Jack, 51
Arendt, Hannah, 132
Arizona, 31, 130
Armed services, 50-51. *See also* Discharge records
Army, 15, 50, 78-92, 126, 155, 156, 200; data system, 14
Arrest records, 13, 16, 93-108, 168ff., 190,

194-98. *See also* FBI; Juvenile Court; Vietnam
Askin, Frank, 147-48
Associated Credit Bureaus, 135
Atlanta, 178
Aware, Inc., 157

Baker, Michael A., 163, 164
Baltimore, 43-45, 109
Baltimore Sun, 43
Barash, Mahlon and Leah, 133
Bassett, James C., 41
Baton Rouge, 131
Bauer, Diane, 44, 45
Beazer, Carl, 58-59, 60
Beaumont, Gustave de, 114-15
Benade, Leo E., 80
Bennett, Daniel, 154
Bentham, Jeremy, 151
Berry, Talmadge, 58
Bertillon system, 121
Bible, Alan, 97, 196
Black Panthers, 150-51
Blacks (Negroes), 52, 61, 103, 104, 131, 156, 178, 179, 180-82, 191. *See also* Race
Blacksheare, Duane, 32
Blood tests, 12, 43-45
Blumenthal, Albert, 75n
Bonaparte, Charles Joseph, 152
Bordier, Nancy, 18
Boston, 186-87
Boy Scouts, 154
Brandeis, Louis D., 189
British, 186, 195, 196-97

• 211

ABOUT THE AUTHOR

Aryeh Neier's concern with civil liberties began almost at birth. He was born in Berlin in 1937 and left Nazi Germany with his parents for England just before war broke out in 1939. When he was ten years old, he emigrated to the United States. He has been the executive director of the American Civil Liberties Union since 1970 and before that served on the ACLU staff and for six years as executive director of the New York State branch. A graduate of Cornell, he has taught at New York University and at the New York City Police Academy. He is coeditor (with Norman Dorsen) of a series of books on people's rights and has contributed to several other books, the most recent of which is *Investigating the FBI* (1973).